The Mediterranean Cookbook

The Mediterranean Cookbook

p

This is a Parragon Publishing Book

This edition published in 2006

Parragon Publishing
Queen Street House
4 Queen Street
Bath BA1 1HE, UK

ISBN: 1-40546-577-8

Printed in China

Produced by the Bridgewater Book Company Ltd

NOTES FOR THE READER

- This book uses imperial, metric, and US cup measurements. Follow the same units of measurement throughout; do not mix imperial and metric.

- All spoon measurements are level: teaspoons are assumed to be 5 ml, and tablespoons are assumed to be 15 ml.

- Unless otherwise stated, milk is assumed to be whole, eggs and individual vegetables such as potatoes are medium, and pepper is freshly ground black pepper.

- Recipes using raw or very lightly cooked eggs should be avoided by infants, the elderly, pregnant women, convalescents, and anyone suffering from an illness.

- Pregnant and breast-feeding women are advised to avoid eating peanuts and peanut products.

- The times given are an approximate guide only. Preparation times differ according to the techniques used by different people and the cooking times may also vary from those given.

Contents

Introduction

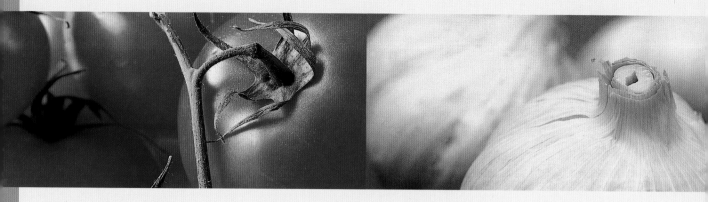

Introduction

8

The beautiful region of the Mediterranean spans a wide and varied area, from sun-drenched coasts and hot, arid plains, to lush green valleys and breathtaking mountains. This diversity brings with it a marvelous variety of foods, with each region able to boast its own famous dishes. However, the various countries that surround the Mediterranean Sea also have one thing in common, and that is the healthiness of their diet.

The health benefits of the Mediterranean diet have long been recognized by health experts—studies by the World Health Organization in 1999 ranked Greece, Spain, Italy, and France among the top ten for life expectancy in the world, and cited the Mediterranean diet as one of the main reasons for this. The diet is low in saturated fat and rich in nutritious grains, beans, vegetables, fruits, olive oil, and seafood. Although Mediterranean people get about 40% of their daily calories from fat, this fat tends to be the healthy variety. They use olive oil, for example, which is a monounsaturated fat, and therefore healthier than saturated animal fats such as butter, which raise cholesterol levels and clog the arteries. Red meat is eaten sparingly, with the emphasis more on lower-fat poultry, and Mediterranean people eat fish regularly, which ensures they get plenty of healthy essential fatty acids.

France—the home of haute cuisine

Mediterranean food is delicious and is popular all over the world. France in particular has long enjoyed a well-deserved reputation for gastronomic excellence, and each of its regions has its own food specialties. In southern France, with its warmer climate, the food is far more Mediterranean than in the cooler northern climes. In Languedoc and Provence, for example, you will find an abundance of olives, as well as garlic, bell peppers, tomatoes, fragrant herbs, and seafood.

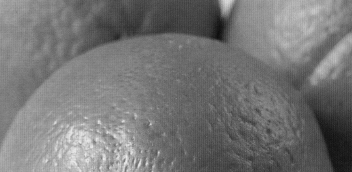

In the Basque region of France, which stretches from the western Pyrenees to the coast, the cooking once again is distinctly Mediterranean, with a liberal use of garlic, olive oil, and tomatoes, as well as some delicious fish dishes.

The French tend to have a light breakfast, which may be just a coffee, sometimes with a croissant or cereal and/or some fruit. A three-course lunch normally makes up for the light breakfast. In the evening, dinner is usually another three-course meal. There may be a salad to start, then an entrée of meat or fish, with vegetables, rice, or French fries, followed by dessert, cake, or cheese.

The marvelous cuisine of Spain

Like France, Spanish cuisine is rich and exciting and differs in each region. In the north, the Basque country is famed for its delicious dishes which feature the freshest fish, such as cod and tuna. Asturias, meanwhile, which has spectacular mountains, green valleys, and rugged coastlines, is famous for salmon, bleu cheeses, and hard cider. The province of Aragon is famous for its "La Rioja" wines, air-cured Teruel hams, and delicious olive oil from Alcañiz. And in Cataluña, you will find excellent sausages, and also sauces such as the famous "alioli."

Moving farther south to Valencia, where the weather is warmer, the region is a patchwork of orchards, rice fields, orange groves, and vineyards. This is the home of the paella, and the region is also famed for its fragrant, juicy oranges. Even farther south, where the summers are very hot and the winters mild, vineyards abound and the orchards are full of avocados, figs, olives, and lemons. The Balearic Islands, meanwhile, are proud of their mayonnaise, pastries, and sausages, while the Canary Islands, the farthest south of all, enjoy a year-round warm climate, which enables them to grow tropical fruits such as bananas.

Breakfast usually comprises coffee and perhaps a pastry or bread roll. There may also be a light snack at mid-morning. Lunch is usually light but unhurried and afterwards many people take a siesta. Around 5 or 6 pm is time for "merienda," which is an afternoon snack, and is also suppertime for children. Like almost all Spanish meals, dinner, taken around 10 pm, tends to be quite light, starting with a soup or omelet and followed by fruit, cheese, or yogurt.

Eating the Italian way

Italian food is delicious, and enjoys an enviable international reputation. In the north of Italy people use more butter, while in the south people use hardly any butter at all—they use olive oil instead.

The northern region of Piedmont has high mountains, soft hills, and lots of vineyards. It also has low, flat fields, ideal for growing rice, so it is no surprise to find risottos are a staple here. Meat and game are stewed in red wine, and the region's wines include the famous Barolo. Bagna cauda is one of the region's signature dishes.

A little farther down, on the east coast, lies the Marche region. It is partly mountainous, with land sloping down to the sea. This region has an abundance of fresh fish and shellfish. Here you will find some outstanding fish soups and popular shellfish dishes such as Mussels Marinara. There are also some delicious pork dishes. Pasta is an important staple throughout Italy and the Marche region is renowned for its long pasta noodles called tagliatelle.

Much farther south lies Campania. The fertile, volcanic soil here produces Italy's finest fruits and vegetables. This is where the gorgeously creamy mozzarella cheese is made and is where the world-famous pizza originated.

Italian meals are leisurely, and can be quite rich, but the portions are usually modest, so you can enjoy this delicious food without feeling you have over-indulged. Appetizers are usually soups, or rice or pasta dishes. Entrées are usually meat or fish with side dishes. Then comes dessert and finally cookies accompanied by strong coffee.

Memorable eating in Greece

Greece has a marvelous climate and its own famous regional dishes. Since it is made up of the mainland and many islands, it has many coastlines, and the fresh fish and shellfish are delicious here. Fried mussels are a specialty in the north.

The northern region of Macedonia, with its extended plains and large rivers, is particularly noted for its fine fruits, tomatoes, eggplants, and okra, and is also renowned for its salads.

In the south, in the Peloponnese region, you will find delicious grapes, figs, and goat cheese. The mouthwatering Chicken with Goat Cheese and Basil echoes the flavors from this region. And on the island of Crete, you will find a marvelous ewe's milk cheese called "Kefalotiri," and a delicacy called "apaki," which is a salt beef covered with spices.

Until the 1960s, meat and other "luxury" foods were out of reach for most Greeks, so the Greek cook learned to create clever and delicious dishes from a few basic ingredients, such as wild greens, cultivated vegetables, lemons, olive oil, onions, and garlic. During this time, the people of Greece enjoyed the longest life expectancy in the world. When the country's economy recovered in the 1960s, however, and meats and imported butter became more widely available, Greece's exemplary record for life expectancy was overtaken by other countries, but it is still one of the top ten countries in the world.

Bringing the flavors of the Mediterranean into your kitchen

Mediterranean food is easy to prepare and uses fresh ingredients that are permitted to speak for themselves. You don't need to stock a lot of special equipment. For example, although some cooks make their own pasta, this is not essential. Commercial brands of fresh pasta are excellent nowadays, and there really isn't any need to make your own. So save your kitchen space for more essential items. If you are going to be making a lot of Spanish paellas, a two-handled paella pan ("paellera") is a great investment, but you can also use a large, shallow skillet if necessary. The main thing is to ensure you have a good selection of the usual cook's utensils, such as sharp knives and different-sized pots and pans.

In your pantry, keep staples such as dried pasta and beans, short-grained risotto rice such as arborio, canned tomatoes, and sun-dried tomatoes. They are ideal for rustling up quick Mediterranean meals. Garlic, olive oil, fresh bell peppers, tomatoes, olives, and herbs are also essentials.

You will find the recipes in this book very easy to prepare and yet delicious to eat. They are timeless classics and capture perfectly the marvelous aromas and flavors of the beautiful Mediterranean.

Soups, Appetizers, and Snacks

SERVES 4–6

1 lb 2 oz/500 g large, juicy tomatoes

3 large, ripe, red bell peppers, cored,
    seeded, and chopped

2–3 tbsp sherry vinegar, to taste

4 tbsp olive oil

pinch of sugar

salt and pepper

TO SERVE

ice cubes

red bell pepper, finely diced

green bell pepper, finely diced

yellow bell pepper, finely diced

seeded cucumber, finely diced

hardcooked eggs, finely chopped

croutons cooked in garlic-flavored
    olive oil

14 GAZPACHO
chilled tomato soup

Remove the stems and cut a small cross in the top of each tomato. Put the tomatoes into a
heatproof bowl, pour over enough boiling water to cover, and leave for 30 seconds. Use a
slotted spoon to transfer to a bowl of ice water. Working with 1 tomato at a time, remove the
skin, then cut in half, and use a teaspoon to scoop out the cores and seeds.

Put the tomatoes, red bell peppers, 2 tablespoons of sherry vinegar, the oil, and sugar in a food
processor and process until blended and as smooth or chunky as you like. Cover with plastic
wrap and chill for at least 4 hours before serving. Taste and adjust the seasoning, adding extra
vinegar if necessary.

To serve, ladle the soup into bowls and add 1 or 2 ice cubes to each. Put a selection of the
garnishes in bowls and let everyone add their own.

COOK'S TIP
Flavors are dulled at cold temperatures, so more seasoning will be needed than for a soup
served warm. For this reason, taste and adjust the seasoning after chilling the soup.

SERVES 4

4 tbsp unsalted butter

4 slices fresh white bread

⅔ cup freshly grated Parmesan cheese

4 eggs

salt and pepper

CONSOMMÉ

1 lb 2 oz/500 g beef marrow bones, sawn
   into 3-inch/7.5-cm pieces

12 oz/350 g stewing beef, in 1 piece

6 cups water

4 cloves

2 onions, halved

2 celery stalks, coarsely chopped

8 peppercorns

1 bouquet garni

ZUPPA PAVESE
beef soup with eggs

First, make the Consommé. Place the bones in a large, heavy-bottomed pot with the stewing beef on top. Add the water and bring to a boil over low heat, skimming off all the scum that rises to the surface. Stick a clove into each onion half and add to the pot with the celery, peppercorns, and bouquet garni. Partially cover and simmer very gently for 3 hours. Remove the meat and simmer for another hour.

Strain the Consommé into a bowl and set aside to cool. When completely cold, cover with plastic wrap and chill in the refrigerator for at least 6 hours, preferably overnight.

Carefully remove and discard the layer of fat that has formed on the surface. Return the Consommé to a clean pot and heat until almost boiling.

When you are ready to serve, melt the butter in a heavy-bottomed skillet. Add the bread, 1 slice at a time if necessary, and cook over medium heat, until crisp and golden on both sides. Remove from the skillet and place one each in the bottom of 4 warmed soup bowls.

Sprinkle half the Parmesan over the cooked bread. Carefully break an egg over each slice of cooked bread, keeping the yolks whole. Season to taste with salt and pepper and sprinkle with the remaining grated Parmesan. Carefully ladle the hot Consommé into the soup bowls and serve immediately.

COOK'S TIP
If you prefer, you could lightly poach the eggs before adding them to the bowls.

SERVES 4–6

1⅔ cups fresh fava beans

2 tbsp olive oil

2 large garlic cloves, crushed

1 large onion, finely chopped

1 celery stalk, finely chopped

1 carrot, peeled and chopped

6 oz/175 g firm new potatoes, such as Charlotte, diced

3½ cups vegetable bouillon

2 large, juicy beefsteak tomatoes, skinned, seeded, and chopped

1 large bunch of fresh basil, tied together with kitchen string

7 oz/200 g zucchini, diced

7 oz/200 g green beans, trimmed and chopped

2 oz/55 g dried vermicelli, broken into pieces, or small dried pasta shapes

salt and pepper

extra-virgin olive oil (optional), to garnish

PISTOU SAUCE

3½ oz/100 g fresh basil leaves

2 large garlic cloves

1½ tbsp pine nuts

generous 3 tbsp fruity extra-virgin olive oil

⅓ cup finely grated Parmesan cheese

SOUPE AU PISTOU

vegetable and bean soup

If the fava beans are young and tender, use them as they are. If they are older, remove the outer skin first: use a knife to slit the skins and "pop" out the beans.

Heat the oil in a large pot with a lid over medium heat. Add the garlic, onion, celery, and carrot and sauté for 5–8 minutes, or until the onion is soft.

Add the potatoes, bouillon, and tomatoes, and season to taste. Bring the bouillon to a boil, skimming the surface if necessary, then add the basil. Lower the heat and cover the pot. Let simmer for 15 minutes, or until the potatoes are tender.

Meanwhile, make the Pistou Sauce. Put the basil, garlic, and pine nuts in a food processor or blender and blitz until a thick paste forms. Add the olive oil and blitz again. Transfer to a bowl and stir in the cheese. Cover with plastic wrap and chill until required.

When the potatoes are tender, stir the fava beans, zucchini, green beans, and vermicelli into the soup, then simmer for 10 minutes, or until the pasta is cooked. Taste and adjust the seasoning if necessary. Remove and discard the basil.

Ladle the soup into bowls and add a spoonful of Pistou Sauce to each bowl. Garnish with a swirl of olive oil, if using.

SERVES 4–6

1 lb 2 oz/500 g day-old country-style
  white bread, crusts removed, then torn

5 large garlic cloves, halved

½ cup extra-virgin olive oil,
  plus a little extra to garnish

4–5 tbsp sherry vinegar, to taste

3⅛ cup ground almonds

5 cups water, chilled

salt and white pepper

seedless white grapes, to garnish

AJO BLANCO
chilled garlic soup

Put the bread in a bowl with just enough cold water to cover and let soak for 15 minutes. Squeeze the bread dry and transfer it to a food processor.

Add the garlic, oil, 4 tablespoons of sherry vinegar, and the ground almonds to the food processor with 1 cup of the water and process until blended.

With the motor running, slowly pour in the remaining water until a smooth soup forms. Taste and add extra sherry vinegar if necessary. Cover with plastic wrap and chill for at least 4 hours.

To serve, stir well and adjust the seasoning if necessary. Ladle into bowls and float grapes on top with a drizzle of olive oil.

SERVES 4

4 large tomatoes

2 tbsp olive oil

1 onion, coarsely chopped

1 garlic clove, chopped

1¼ cups vegetable bouillon

2 ready-to-eat sun-dried
  tomatoes, chopped

1 tsp chopped fresh thyme

½ tsp ground cinnamon

1¼ cups strained plain yogurt

salt and pepper

SOÚPA YAOÚRTI-DOMÁTA
yogurt and tomato soup

Coarsely grate the tomatoes into a bowl, discarding the skins left in your hand. Heat the oil in a pot, add the onion and garlic, and cook over low heat for 5 minutes, or until softened. Add the tomatoes and cook gently for another 5 minutes.

Add the bouillon, sun-dried tomatoes, thyme, cinnamon, and salt and pepper. Bring to a boil, then simmer for 10 minutes.

Remove from the heat, let the soup cool slightly, then purée in a food processor or blender, or use a hand-held blender. Add the yogurt and mix together. Adjust the seasoning, if necessary.

If serving hot, reheat the soup gently. (Do not boil, or the soup will curdle.) If serving cold, let cool, cover with plastic wrap, and then chill in the refrigerator for 3–4 hours.

SERVES 4

1 tbsp olive oil

1 lb 7 oz/650 g plum tomatoes

1 onion, cut into fourths

1 garlic clove, thinly sliced

1 celery stalk, coarsely chopped

2 cups chicken bouillon

2 oz/55 g dried anellini or other
   soup pasta

salt and pepper

fresh flatleaf parsley, chopped,
   to garnish

ZUPPA DI POMODORI

fresh tomato soup

Pour the olive oil into a large, heavy-bottomed pot and add the tomatoes, onion, garlic, and celery. Cover and cook over low heat for 45 minutes, occasionally shaking the pot gently, until the mixture is pulpy.

Transfer the mixture to a food processor or blender and process to a smooth purée. Push the purée through a strainer into a clean pot.

Add the bouillon and bring to a boil. Add the pasta, bring back to a boil, and cook for 8–10 minutes, or until the pasta is tender but still firm to the bite. Season to taste with salt and pepper. Ladle into warmed bowls, sprinkle with the parsley, and serve immediately.

SERVES 4–6

2 large tomatoes

3–4 tbsp olive oil

1 large onion, finely chopped

1 large red bell pepper, cored, seeded, and chopped

1 large green bell pepper, cored, seeded, and chopped

2 oz/55 g chorizo sausage, thinly sliced, casings removed, if preferred

generous 2 tbsp unsalted butter

10 large eggs, lightly beaten

salt and pepper

4–6 thick slices country-style bread, toasted, to serve

PIPERRADA
basque scrambled eggs

Remove the stems and cut a small cross in the top of each tomato. Put the tomatoes into a heatproof bowl, pour over enough boiling water to cover, and let stand for 30 seconds. Use a slotted spoon to transfer to a bowl of ice water. Working with 1 tomato at a time, remove the skin, then cut in half and use a teaspoon to scoop out the cores and seeds.

Heat 2 tablespoons of oil in a large, heavy-bottomed skillet over medium-high heat. Add the onion and bell peppers and cook for 5 minutes, or until the vegetables are soft but not brown. Add the tomatoes and heat through. Transfer to a plate and keep warm in a preheated low oven.

Add another tablespoon of oil to the skillet. Add the chorizo and cook for 30 seconds, just to warm through and flavor the oil. Add the sausage to the reserved vegetables.

There should be about 2 tablespoons of oil in the skillet. If not, add a little extra to make up to that amount. Add the butter and melt over low heat. Season the eggs with salt and pepper, then add to the skillet and scramble until cooked to the desired degree of firmness. Return the vegetables to the pan and stir through. Serve immediately, with hot toast.

SERVES 4

6–8 slices French bread or other
  crusty bread

3–4 tomatoes, halved

1–2 garlic cloves (optional)

olive oil, for drizzling (optional)

PA AMB TOMÀQUET
tomato bread

To serve this at its simplest, simply rub the slices of bread with the tomato halves, letting the juice and seeds soak into the bread. If the bread is soft, you can toast it first. Other options are to flavor it with garlic in the same way, or drizzle olive oil over the top of the tomato.

VARIATION

To make Pan con Tomate, a more substantial snack, serve it with a plate of thinly sliced serrano ham and Manchego cheese, and let guests assemble open sandwiches. (If unavailable, you can use prosciutto and romano cheese instead. Although these are not traditional Catalan ingredients, they work just as well.)

MAKES ABOUT 10½ oz/300 g

9 oz/250 g black olives, such as Nyons
   or niçoise, pitted

3 anchovy fillets in oil, drained

1 large garlic clove, halved, with the
   green center removed, if necessary

2 tbsp pine nuts

½ tbsp capers in brine, rinsed

½ cup extra-virgin olive oil

freshly squeezed lemon or orange juice,
   to taste

pepper

GARLIC CROUTES

12 slices French bread or other crusty
   bread, about ¼ inch/5 mm thick

extra-virgin olive oil, for brushing

2 garlic cloves, peeled but left whole

TAPENADE
black olive paste

Put the olives, anchovy fillets, garlic, pine nuts, and capers in a food processor or blender and whizz until well blended. With the motor still running, pour the olive oil through the feed tube and continue blending until a loose paste forms.

Add the lemon juice and pepper to taste. It shouldn't need any salt because of the saltiness of the anchovies. Transfer to a bowl, cover with plastic wrap, and chill until required.

To make the Garlic Croûtes, preheat the broiler to high. Place the bread slices on the broiler rack and broil one side for 1–2 minutes, or until golden brown. Flip the bread slices over, lightly brush the uncooked side with olive oil, then broil for 1–2 minutes.

Rub 1 side of each bread slice with garlic while it is still hot, then set aside and let cool completely. Store in an airtight container for up to 2 days.

Serve the tapenade with the Garlic Croûtes.

COOK'S TIP

Any leftover tapenade can be stored in a covered container in the refrigerator for up to a week. Pour a thin layer of olive oil over the surface before covering.

SERVES 8

1 cup garbanzo beans, covered with
   water and soaked overnight
juice of 2 large lemons
⅔ cup sesame seed paste
2 garlic cloves, crushed
4 tbsp extra-virgin olive oil
small pinch of ground cumin
salt and pepper

TO GARNISH

1 tsp paprika
flatleaf parsley, chopped

warm pitas, to serve

HÚMMOUS KAI TACHÍNI
garbanzo bean and sesame dip

Drain the garbanzo beans, put in a pan, and cover with cold water. Bring to a boil, then simmer for 2 hours, or until very tender.

Drain the garbanzo beans, reserving a little of the liquid, and put in a food processor, reserving a few to garnish. Blend the garbanzo beans until smooth, gradually adding the lemon juice and enough reserved liquid to form a smooth, thick purée. Add the sesame seed paste, garlic, 3 tablespoons of the olive oil, and the cumin, and blend until smooth. Season with salt and pepper.

Turn the mixture into a shallow serving dish, cover with plastic wrap, and chill in the refrigerator for 2–3 hours before serving. To serve, mix the remaining olive oil with the paprika and drizzle over the top of the dish. Sprinkle with the parsley and the reserved garbanzo beans. Accompany with warm pitas.

SERVES 6

8 oz/225 g smoked cod roe or fresh red
   snapper roe

1 small onion, cut into fourths

1 cup fresh white bread crumbs

1 large garlic clove, crushed

grated rind and juice of 1 large lemon

⅔ cup extra-virgin olive oil

6 tbsp hot water

pepper

TO GARNISH

black olives, preferably Greek

capers

flatleaf parsley, chopped

crackers, potato chips, or pitas,
   to serve

TARAMASALÁTA
smoked cod roe dip

Remove the skin from the fish roe. Put the onion in a food processor and chop finely. Add the cod roe in small pieces and blend until smooth. Add the bread crumbs, garlic, lemon rind, and lemon juice, and mix together well.

With the machine running, very slowly pour in the oil. When all the oil has been added, blend in the water. Season with pepper.

Turn the mixture into a serving bowl, cover with plastic wrap, and chill in the refrigerator for at least 1 hour before serving. Serve garnished with olives, capers, and chopped parsley, and accompany with crackers, potato chips, or pitas.

SERVES 4

1 small cucumber

1¼ cups strained plain yogurt

1 large garlic clove, crushed

1 tbsp chopped fresh mint or dill

salt and pepper

warm pitas, to serve

TZATZÍKI

cucumber and yogurt dip

Peel and then coarsely grate the cucumber. Put in a strainer and squeeze out as much of the water as possible by pressing with the back of a spoon. Put the cucumber into a bowl.

Add the yogurt, garlic, and chopped mint (reserve a little as a garnish, if you desire) to the cucumber and season with pepper. Mix well together, cover with plastic wrap, and chill in the refrigerator for about 2 hours before serving.

To serve, stir the Cucumber and Yogurt Dip and transfer to a serving bowl. Sprinkle with salt and accompany with warm pitas.

SERVES 4

7 oz/200 g beef tenderloin, in 1 piece

2 tbsp lemon juice

4 tbsp extra-virgin olive oil

⅓ cup thinly shaved
  Parmesan cheese

4 tbsp chopped fresh flatleaf parsley

salt and pepper

lemon slices, to garnish

ciabatta or focaccia, to serve

38 CARPACCIO
marinated raw beef

Using a very sharp knife, cut the beef tenderloin into wafer-thin slices and arrange on 4 individual serving plates.

Pour the lemon juice into a small bowl and season to taste with salt and pepper. Whisk in the olive oil, then pour the dressing over the meat. Cover the plates with plastic wrap and set aside for 10–15 minutes to marinate.

Remove and discard the plastic wrap. Arrange the Parmesan shavings in the center of each serving and sprinkle with parsley. Garnish with lemon slices and serve with fresh bread.

VARIATION
To make Carpaccio di Tonno, substitute fresh, uncooked tuna for the beef tenderloin. Do not use thawed frozen fish. Eat on the day of purchase.

MAKES ABOUT 16

7 oz/200 g Manchego cheese, in
  one piece
1 cup fresh, fine, white bread crumbs
1 tsp dried thyme
1 large egg
olive oil, for pan-frying
few sprigs of fresh thyme, to garnish

ROMESCO SAUCE (OPTIONAL)

4 large, ripe tomatoes
16 blanched almonds
3 large garlic cloves, unpeeled and
  left whole
1 dried sweet chili, such as ñora, soaked
  for 20 minutes and patted dry
4 dried red chilies, soaked for
  20 minutes and patted dry
pinch of sugar
⅔ cup extra-virgin olive oil
2 tbsp red wine vinegar
salt and pepper

40

QUESO FRITO
fried cheese

If you are making the Romesco Sauce, preheat the oven to 350°F/180°C. Place the tomatoes, almonds, and garlic on a cookie sheet, and roast in the oven for 20 minutes, but check the almonds after about 7 minutes because they can burn quickly; remove as soon as they are golden and giving off an aroma.

Remove from the oven, and peel the roasted garlic and tomatoes. Put the almonds, garlic, sweet chili, and dried red chilies in a food processor and process until finely chopped. Add the tomatoes and sugar and process again. With the motor running, slowly add the olive oil through the feed tube. Add 1½ tablespoons of the vinegar and quickly process. Taste and add extra vinegar, if desired, and salt and pepper to taste, and set aside.

De-rind the cheese, then cut it into 16 wedge-shaped slices, each ¼–½ inch/0.5–1 cm thick; set aside. Mix the bread crumbs and thyme together on a plate and beat the egg in a shallow soup bowl. Dip the cheese wedges one by one, first in egg, then in bread crumbs, patting the wedges all over.

Heat ¼ inch/5 mm of oil in a heavy-bottomed skillet to 350–375°F/150–190°C, or until a cube of day-old bread browns in 30 seconds. Add the cheese wedges and cook for 30 seconds on each side, or until golden brown and crisp. Work in batches, if necessary, to avoid over-crowding the skillet.

As each wedge is cooked, remove it from the skillet and drain on paper towels. Let cool slightly, then serve garnished with thyme, and the sauce for dipping, if using.

SERVES 4

2 lb 4 oz/1 kg fresh spinach, tough
   stalks removed
generous 1½ cups ricotta cheese
⅔ cup freshly grated Parmesan cheese
3 eggs, lightly beaten
pinch of freshly grated nutmeg

generous ⅞–1¾ cups all-purpose flour,
   plus extra for dusting
salt and pepper

HERB BUTTER
½ cup unsalted butter
2 tbsp chopped fresh oregano
2 tbsp chopped fresh sage

spinach and ricotta dumplings

Rinse the spinach, shake dry, then place it in a pan with only the water that clings to its leaves. Cover and cook over low heat for 6–8 minutes, or until just wilted. Drain well and set aside to cool.

Put the spinach in a strainer and use a potato masher to press out all the liquid from the spinach, then chop finely or process in a food processor or blender. Place the spinach in a bowl and add the ricotta, half the Parmesan, the eggs, nutmeg, and seasoning. Beat until combined. Sift in ⅞ cup of the flour and work it into the mixture, adding more, if necessary, to make a workable mixture. Cover with plastic wrap and chill for 1 hour.

With floured hands, break off small pieces of the mixture and roll them into walnut-size balls. Lightly dust the dumplings with flour.

Bring a large pan of lightly salted water to a boil. Add the dumplings and cook for about 2–3 minutes, or until they rise to the surface. Remove them from the pan with a slotted spoon, drain well, and set aside.

Meanwhile, make the Herb Butter. Melt the butter in a large, heavy-bottomed skillet. Add the oregano and sage and cook over low heat, stirring frequently, for 1 minute. Add the dumplings and toss gently for 1 minute to coat. Transfer to a warmed serving dish, sprinkle with the remaining Parmesan, and serve.

MAKES ABOUT 30

8-oz/225-g package grape leaves
   preserved in brine
generous ½ cup arborio rice, or other
   short-grain rice
¾ cup olive oil
1 small onion, finely chopped
1 garlic clove, finely chopped
⅓ cup pine nuts, chopped
⅓ cup currants
3 scallions, finely chopped

1 tbsp chopped fresh mint
1 tbsp chopped fresh dill
2 tbsp chopped fresh flatleaf parsley
juice of 1 lemon
⅔ cup water
salt and pepper

TO SERVE
lemon wedges
strained plain yogurt

44 DOLMÁDES
stuffed grape leaves

Place the grape leaves in a large bowl, pour over boiling water, and let soak for 20 minutes. Drain, soak in cold water for 20 minutes, and then drain again.

Meanwhile, put the rice and a pinch of salt in a pan. Cover with cold water and bring to a boil, then simmer for 15–20 minutes, or as directed on the package, until tender. Drain well, transfer to a bowl, and set aside to cool.

Heat 2 tablespoons of the oil in a large, heavy-bottomed skillet, add the onion and garlic, and cook for 5–10 minutes, or until softened. Add the onions to the rice with the pine nuts, currants, scallions, mint, dill, and parsley. Season with a little salt and plenty of pepper and mix the ingredients together well.

Place 1 grape leaf, vein-side upward, on a counter. Put a little filling on the bottom of the leaf and fold up the bottom end of the leaf. Fold the opposite sides of the leaf into the center, then roll up the leaf around the filling. Squeeze the parcel gently in your hand to seal. Fill and roll the grape leaves until all the ingredients have been used up, putting any torn leaves in the bottom of a large, flameproof casserole. Put the stuffed leaves, seam-side down and in a single layer, in the casserole, packing them as close together as possible.

Mix the remaining oil and the lemon juice with ⅔ cup water and pour into the casserole. Place a large plate over the grape leaves to keep them in place, then cover the casserole with a lid. Bring to simmering point, then simmer for 45 minutes. Leave the grape leaves to cool in the liquid. Serve warm or chilled, with lemon wedges and yogurt.

MAKES 25

2 tbsp olive oil

25 pieces of chorizo sausage,
  each about ½ inch/1 cm square
  (about 3½ oz/100 g)

25 white mushrooms, wiped and
  stalks removed

1 large green bell pepper, broiled and
  skinned (see Cook's Tip), and cut into
  25 squares

PINCHITOS DE CHORIZO Y CHAMPIÑONES

chorizo and mushroom kabobs

Heat the oil in a skillet over medium-high heat. Add the chorizo and cook for 20 seconds, stirring. Add the mushrooms and continue cooking for another 1–2 minutes, or until the mushrooms begin to brown and absorb the fat in the skillet.

Thread a green bell pepper square, a piece of chorizo, and a mushroom onto a wooden toothpick. Continue until all the ingredients are used. Serve hot or at room temperature.

COOK'S TIP

To skin bell peppers, halve lengthwise, stem on, which makes removal of the core and seeds simpler. Broil, skin-sides up, 2–3 inches/5–7.5 cm from the heat, until charred all over. Remove from the heat and place in a plastic bag for 15 minutes, then rub or peel off the skins. Remove any cores and seeds. Alternatively, the peppers can be charred over a flame. Broiled and skinned peppers can be covered with olive oil and kept for up to 5 days in the refrigerator.

SERVES 6–8

9 oz/250 g shortcrust pie dough, thawed if frozen

6 tbsp garlic-flavored olive oil

2 lb 4 oz/1 kg onions, thinly sliced

½ tbsp dried thyme leaves

5 tbsp black olive paste (Tapenade)

salt and pepper

TO GARNISH

2 oz/55 g anchovy fillets in oil, drained and sliced lengthwise

12–15 black olives, pitted

PISSALADIÈRE
anchovy and onion tart

Preheat the oven to 400°F/200°C, with a cookie sheet inside. Roll out the pie dough on a lightly floured counter and use to line a 11 x 8-inch/28 x 20-cm rectangular tart pan. Gently roll a rolling pin over the top of the pan to take off the excess pie dough. Line with waxed paper and fill with pie weights. Put the tart shell on the hot cookie sheet and bake for 10–15 minutes, or until the rim is set. Remove the paper and weights, then return the tart shell to the oven, and bake for another 5 minutes, or until the bottom looks dry.

Meanwhile, heat the oil in a large, heavy-bottomed skillet with a tight-fitting lid over medium-high heat. Add the onions and stir until coated in oil.

Lower the heat to the lowest setting. Press a wet piece of waxed paper over the surface, then cover with the lid. Leave the onions to simmer for 45 minutes, or until tender. Remove the paper, stir in the thyme, and season, remembering the anchovies are salty.

Meanwhile, reheat the oven to 350°F/180°C. Spread the black olive paste over the bottom of the tart shell. Spoon the onions into the tart shell and spread out evenly. Arrange the anchovy fillets in a lattice pattern on top and dot with the olives.

Return the tart to the oven and bake for 25–30 minutes, or until the crust is golden. If the crust begins to brown too much, cover the tart with a sheet of foil. Transfer the tart to a wire rack and let stand for 10 minutes before removing from the pan. Let cool completely, then cut into slices.

SERVES 4–6

2½ oz/70 g sea salt

24 small, new red-skinned potatoes,
  unpeeled and kept whole

MOJO SAUCE

1½ oz/40 g day-old bread, crusts
  removed, then torn into small pieces

2 large garlic cloves

½ tsp salt

1½ tbsp hot Spanish paprika

1 tbsp ground cumin

2–3 tbsp red wine vinegar, to taste

5–6 tbsp extra-virgin olive oil

2 pimientos del piquillo (preserved red
  bell pepper pieces), drained

PAPAS ARRAGUADAS CON MOJO

"wrinkled" potatoes with mojo sauce

Pour about 1 inch/2.5 cm water in a pan and stir in the sea salt. Add the potatoes and stir again: they do not have to be covered with water. Fold a clean dish towel to fit over the potatoes, then bring the water to a boil. Lower the heat and simmer for 20 minutes, or until the potatoes are tender but still holding together. Remove the dish towel and set aside.

Drain the potatoes and return them to the pan. When the dish towel is cool enough to handle, wring out the saltwater into the pan. Put the pan over low heat and shake until the potatoes are dry and coated with a thin, white film. Remove from the heat.

Meanwhile, make the Mojo Sauce. Put the bread in a bowl and add just enough water to cover; set aside for 5 minutes to soften. Use your hands to squeeze all the water from the bread. Use a pestle and mortar to mash the garlic and salt into a paste. Stir in the paprika and cumin. Transfer the mixture to a food processor. Add 2 tablespoons of vinegar and blend, then add the bread and 2 tablespoons of oil and blend again.

With the motor running, add the bell pepper pieces a few at a time until they are puréed and a sauce forms. Add more oil, if necessary, until the sauce is smooth and thick. Taste and adjust the seasoning, adding extra vinegar, if necessary.

To serve, cut the potatoes in half and spear with wooden toothpicks. Serve with a bowl of sauce on the side for dipping. The potatoes can be eaten hot or at room temperature.

Meat and Poultry

SERVES 6–8

2 pinches of saffron threads

4 tbsp hot water

2 cups Spanish short-grain rice

16 raw shrimp

16 live mussels

6 tbsp olive oil

6–8 unboned chicken thighs, excess fat removed, skin left on

5 oz/140 g chorizo sausage, cut into ¼-inch/5-mm slices, casings removed

2 large onions, chopped

4 large garlic cloves, crushed

1 tsp mild or hot Spanish paprika

3½ oz/100 g green beans, chopped

⅔ cup frozen peas

5 cups fish, chicken, or vegetable bouillon

2 sweet red bell peppers, broiled, skinned, cored, seeded and sliced

generous ½ cup finely chopped fresh parsley

salt and pepper

54 PAELLA
paella

Put the saffron in a bowl and add 4 tablespoons of hot water; set aside. Put the rice in a strainer and rinse thoroughly; set aside. Peel the shrimp, cut a slit along the back of each, and remove and discard the dark vein, then reserve until required. Scrub the mussels, removing any beards, and discard any with cracked shells or open ones that do not close when tapped. Set aside.

Heat 3 tablespoons of oil in a 12-inch/30-cm paella pan or flameproof casserole over medium-high heat. Add the chicken thighs, skin-sides down, and cook for 5 minutes, or until golden and crispy. Transfer to a bowl. Add the chorizo to the paella pan and cook for 1 minute, or until it starts to crisp. Add it to the chicken.

Heat another 3 tablespoons of oil in the paella pan. Add the onions and cook for 2 minutes, then add the garlic and paprika and cook for another 3 minutes, or until the onions are soft but not brown. Add the rice, beans, and peas to the paella pan, and stir until coated in oil. Return the chicken thighs and chorizo and any accumulated juices to the casserole. Stir in the bouillon, saffron liquid, and salt and pepper and bring to a boil, stirring.

Lower the heat and simmer, without stirring, for 15 minutes, or until the rice is almost tender and most of the liquid is absorbed. Arrange the mussels, shrimp, and bell pepper strips on top, cover the casserole, and simmer, without stirring, for 5 minutes, or until the shrimp become pink and the mussels open. Discard any mussels that do not open. Taste and adjust the seasoning. Sprinkle with the parsley and serve immediately.

SERVES 4

4 boneless chicken breast portions,
   about 6 oz/175 g each
2 tbsp unsalted butter
1 tbsp sunflower oil
salt and pepper

TARRAGON SAUCE

2 tbsp tarragon-flavored vinegar
6 tbsp dry white wine, such as Muscadet
1 cup chicken bouillon
4 sprigs of fresh tarragon, plus 2 tbsp
   chopped fresh tarragon
1¼ cups crème fraîche or sour cream

56 POULET SAUCE ESTRAGON
chicken in tarragon sauce

Preheat the oven to 375°F/190°C. Season the chicken breast portions on both sides with salt and pepper. Melt the butter with the oil in a skillet large enough to hold the chicken pieces in a single layer, over medium-high heat. Add the chicken breast portions, skin-sides down, and cook for 3–5 minutes, or until golden brown.

Transfer the chicken breasts to a roasting pan and roast for 15–20 minutes, or until they are tender and the juices run clear when a skewer is inserted into the thickest part of the meat. Transfer the chicken to a serving platter, cover with foil, shiny-sides down, and set aside.

To make the Tarragon Sauce, tilt the roasting pan and use a metal spoon to remove the excess fat from the surface of the cooking juices. Place the pan over medium-high heat and add the vinegar, scraping any sediment from the bottom of the pan. Pour in the wine and bring to a boil, still stirring and scraping, and boil until the liquid is reduced by half.

Stir in the bouillon and whole tarragon sprigs and continue boiling until the liquid reduces by about half again. Stir in the crème fraîche and continue boiling to reduce all the liquid by half. Discard the tarragon sprigs and adjust the seasoning if necessary. Stir the chopped tarragon into the sauce.

To serve, slice the chicken breasts on individual plates and spoon one fourth of the Tarragon Sauce over each.

SERVES 4

4 chicken breast fillets, skinned

scant ½ cup soft goat cheese

small bunch fresh basil

2 tbsp olive oil

salt and pepper

KOTÓPOULO ME TIRÍ PRÓVIO KAI VASILIKÓ
chicken with goat cheese and basil

Using a sharp knife, slit along one long edge of each chicken breast fillet, then carefully open out each one to make a small pocket. Divide the cheese equally among the pockets and tuck 3–4 basil leaves in each. Close the openings and season the breast portions with salt and pepper.

Heat the oil in a skillet, add the chicken breast fillets, and cook gently for 15–20 minutes, turning several times, until golden and tender. Serve warm, garnished with sprigs of basil.

SERVES 4

1⅓ cups fresh or frozen shelled fava
  beans

2–3 tbsp olive oil

8 unboned chicken thighs, excess fat
  removed, skin left on

1 large onion, thinly sliced

1 large garlic clove, crushed

1 lb 2 oz/500 g crimini mushrooms,
  wiped and thickly sliced

2 cups chicken bouillon

salt and pepper

fresh parsley, finely chopped, to garnish

fried potatoes, to serve

MUSLOS DE POLLO CON HABAS Y CHAMPIÑONES

chicken thighs with fava beans and mushrooms

To blanch the beans, bring a large pan of salted water to a boil, add the beans, and continue boiling for 5–10 minutes, or until just tender. Drain and put in a bowl of cold water to stop them from cooking farther. Peel off the outer skins and set aside.

Heat 2 tablespoons of oil in a lidded skillet or flameproof casserole over medium heat. Add 4 chicken thighs, skin-sides down; cook for 5 minutes, or until the skins are crisp. Remove from the pan; keep warm. Cook the remaining thighs, adding more oil if needed.

Drain off all but 2 tablespoons of the fat in the pan. Add the onion and cook for 3 minutes; add the garlic and cook for 5 minutes, or until the onion is golden. Stir in the mushrooms and seasoning to taste and cook for 2 minutes, or until the mushrooms give off their juices.

Return the chicken thighs to the pan, skin-sides up. Pour in the bouillon and bring to a boil. Lower the heat, cover, and simmer for 15 minutes. Add the beans and simmer for 5 minutes, or until the beans are tender and the chicken juices run clear when a thigh is pierced. Taste and adjust the seasoning. Sprinkle with parsley and serve with fried potatoes.

SERVES 8–10

1 veal knuckle

4 lb/1.8 kg chicken

1 lb 9 oz/700 g rump of beef

6 black peppercorns

2 bay leaves

1 tbsp shredded fresh basil leaves

2 tsp fresh thyme leaves

small white cabbage, cut into fourths, thick stem removed

2 celery stalks, coarsely chopped

2 leeks, coarsely chopped

1 lb/450 g carrots, sliced

12 pearl onions or shallots

2 lb 4 oz/1 kg potatoes, peeled and sliced

1 cotechino or an 8–12-inch/20–30-cm piece of cooking sausage, such as luganega

salt and pepper

TO SERVE

gherkins

pickled pearl onions

mostarda di Cremona (optional)

salad greens

BOLLITO MISTO
mixed meat stew

Place the veal knuckle in a very large, heavy-bottomed pot. Half-fill the pot with water, add a good pinch of salt, and bring to a boil. Skim off any scum that rises to the surface, then boil for 45 minutes.

Add the chicken, beef, peppercorns, bay leaves, basil, and thyme to the pot and cover, then lower the heat and simmer for 1½ hours.

Add the cabbage, celery, leeks, carrots, onions, potatoes, and sausage to the pot. If necessary, add more water to cover the vegetables. Bring back to a boil over medium heat, then lower the heat, and simmer for another hour, or until the meat and vegetables are tender. Check the seasoning and adjust if necessary.

Remove and discard the veal knuckle and the bay leaves. Transfer the beef, chicken, and cotechino to a cutting board. Carve the beef into slices and cut the chicken into pieces. Slice the sausage into bite-size pieces. Arrange all the meat down the center of a warmed serving platter.

Using a slotted spoon, arrange the vegetables around the meat. Spoon 4–5 tablespoons of the cooking liquid over the meat and serve immediately with gherkins, pickled pearl onions, mostarda di Cremona (if using), and salad greens.

COOK'S TIP
The richly flavored cooking liquid is traditionally served on its own as a separate soup course.

SERVES 4

1 lb/450 g lean, finely ground lamb

1 onion

1 garlic clove, crushed

½ cup fresh white or brown
    bread crumbs

1 tbsp chopped fresh mint

1 tbsp chopped fresh parsley

1 egg, beaten

salt and pepper

olive oil, for brushing

freshly cooked rice or warm pitas,
    to serve

KEFTÉDES
grecian meatballs

Put the ground lamb in a bowl. Grate in the onion, then add the garlic, bread crumbs, mint, and parsley. Season well with salt and pepper. Mix the ingredients well, then add the beaten egg and mix to bind the mixture together. Alternatively, the ingredients can be mixed in a food processor.

With damp hands, form the mixture into 16 small balls and thread onto 4 flat metal skewers. Lightly oil a broiler pan and brush the meatballs with oil.

Preheat the broiler and cook the meatballs under medium heat for 10 minutes, turning frequently and brushing with more oil if necessary, until browned. Serve the meatballs with rice or tucked into warm pitas.

SERVES 4

juice of 2 large lemons

generous ⅓ cup olive oil

1 garlic clove, crushed

1 tbsp chopped fresh oregano or mint

1 lb 9 oz/700 g boned leg or fillet
  of lamb

2 green bell peppers

2 zucchini

12 pearl onions

8 large bay leaves

salt and pepper

lemon wedges, to garnish

TO SERVE

freshly cooked rice

Cucumber and Yogurt Dip (Tzatzíki)

66

SOUVLÁKIA
marinated lamb and vegetable kabobs

Put the lemon juice, oil, garlic, and oregano in a bowl and whisk together. Season with salt and pepper. Trim and cut the lamb into 1½-inch/4-cm cubes and add to the marinade.

Toss the lamb in the marinade, cover with plastic wrap, and chill in the refrigerator overnight or for at least 8 hours. Stir occasionally to coat the lamb.

When ready to serve, core and seed the bell peppers and cut into 1¼-inch/3-cm cubes. Cut the zucchini into 1-inch/2.5-cm pieces. Thread the lamb, bell peppers, zucchini, onions, and bay leaves onto 8 flat, greased, metal kabob skewers, alternating and dividing the ingredients as evenly as possible. Place on a greased broiler pan.

Preheat the broiler, then put the kabobs under the broiler, and cook for 10–15 minutes, turning frequently and basting with any remaining marinade, until cooked. Serve hot on a bed of rice, garnished with lemon wedges, with a bowl of Tzatzíki.

SERVES 4

4 tbsp strained plain yogurt

grated zest of 1 lemon

2 garlic cloves, crushed

3 tbsp olive oil

1 tsp ground cumin

1 lb 10 oz/700 g lean boneless
  lamb, cubed

1 onion, thinly sliced

⅔ cup dry white wine

1 lb/450 g tomatoes, coarsely chopped

1 tbsp tomato paste

pinch of sugar

2 tbsp chopped fresh oregano or
  1 tsp dried

2 bay leaves

3 oz/85 g kalamata olives

14 oz/400 g canned artichoke hearts,
  drained and halved

salt and pepper

ARNÍ ME DOMÁTES, ANGINÁRES KAI ELIÉS

lamb with tomatoes, artichokes, and olives

Put the yogurt, lemon zest, garlic, 1 tablespoon of the olive oil, and the cumin in a large bowl and mix together. Season with salt and pepper. Add the lamb and toss together until coated in the mixture. Cover and let marinate for at least 1 hour.

Heat 1 tablespoon of the olive oil in a large flameproof casserole. Add the lamb in batches and cook for about 5 minutes, stirring frequently, until browned on all sides. Using a slotted spoon, remove the meat from the casserole. Add the remaining tablespoon of oil to the casserole with the onion and cook for 5 minutes, or until softened.

Pour the wine into the casserole, stirring in any glazed bits from the bottom, and bring to a boil. Lower the heat and return the meat to the casserole, then stir in the tomatoes, tomato paste, sugar, oregano, and bay leaves.

Cover the casserole with a lid and simmer for 1½ hours, or until the lamb is tender. Stir in the olives and artichokes and simmer for another 10 minutes. Serve hot.

SERVES 4–6

2 tbsp olive oil

12 merguez sausages

2 onions, finely chopped

2 red bell peppers, cored, seeded, and chopped

1 orange or yellow bell pepper, cored, seeded, and chopped

1⅓ cups small green lentils, rinsed

1 tsp dried thyme or marjoram

scant 2 cups vegetable bouillon

4 tbsp chopped fresh parsley

salt and pepper

red wine vinegar, to serve

SALCHICHAS MERGUEZ CON LENTEJAS
sausages with lentils

Heat the oil in a large, preferably nonstick, lidded skillet over medium-high heat. Add the sausages and cook, stirring frequently, for 10 minutes, or until they are brown all over and cooked through. Remove the sausages from the skillet and set aside.

Pour off all but 2 tablespoons of fat from the pan. Add the onions and bell peppers and cook for 5 minutes, or until soft but not brown. Add the lentils and thyme and stir until coated with oil.

Stir in the bouillon and bring to a boil. Lower the heat, cover, and simmer for 30 minutes, or until the lentils are tender and the liquid is absorbed; if the lentils are tender but too much liquid remains, uncover the pan and simmer until it evaporates. Season to taste with salt and pepper.

Return the sausages to the pan and reheat. Stir in the parsley. Serve the sausages with lentils on the side, then splash a little red wine vinegar over each portion.

COOK'S TIP
Merguez are small, spiced, uncooked sausages from Algeria, and are made with lamb or beef. If you can't find them, use thin Italian sausages instead, flavored with a little paprika, cumin, and chili powder.

SERVES 4

1 tbsp extra-virgin olive oil

4 tbsp butter

2 onions, chopped

1 leek, chopped

3 tbsp all-purpose flour

4 thick slices of veal shank (osso buco)

1¼ cups white wine

1¼ cups veal bouillon or
   chicken bouillon

salt and pepper

GREMOLATA

2 tbsp chopped fresh parsley

1 garlic clove, finely chopped

grated zest of 1 lemon

OSSO BUCO
milanese veal

Heat the oil and butter in a large, heavy-bottomed skillet. Add the onions and leek and cook over low heat, stirring occasionally, for 5 minutes, or until softened.

Spread out the flour on a plate and season with salt and pepper. Toss the pieces of veal in the flour to coat, shaking off any excess. Add the veal to the pan, increase the heat to high, and cook until browned on both sides.

Gradually stir in the wine and bouillon and bring just to a boil, stirring constantly. Lower the heat, cover, and simmer for 1¼ hours, or until the veal is very tender.

Meanwhile, make the Gremolata by mixing the parsley, garlic, and lemon zest in a small bowl.

Use a slotted spoon to transfer the veal to a warmed serving dish. Bring the sauce to a boil and cook, stirring occasionally, until thickened and reduced. Pour the sauce over the veal, sprinkle with the Gremolata, and serve immediately.

VARIATION

Alternative versions of this dish often include tomatoes. If you like, add 14 oz/400 g canned tomatoes along with the wine and bouillon. You could also add in 1 finely chopped carrot and 1 finely chopped celery stalk with the onions and leek.

SERVES 4

1 lb 9 oz/700 g tomatoes, skinned and chopped

3 tbsp olive oil, plus extra for brushing

1 red bell pepper, cored, seeded, and chopped

1 onion, chopped

2 garlic cloves, finely chopped

1 tbsp chopped fresh flatleaf parsley

1 tsp dried oregano

1 tsp sugar

4 sirloin or round steaks, about 6 oz/175 g each

salt and pepper

BISTECCA ALLA PIZZAIOLA
chargrilled steak with tomatoes and garlic

To skin and seed tomatoes, remove the stems and cut a small cross in the top of each one. Put the tomatoes into a heatproof bowl, pour over enough boiling water to cover, and let stand for 30 seconds. Use a slotted spoon to transfer to a bowl of ice water. Working with 1 tomato at a time, remove the skin, then cut in half and use a teaspoon to scoop out the cores and seeds.

Place the oil, tomatoes, red bell pepper, onion, garlic, parsley, oregano, and sugar in a heavy-bottomed pan and season to taste with salt and pepper. Bring to a boil, lower the heat, and simmer for 15 minutes.

Meanwhile, preheat a grill pan over high heat. Trim any fat from the steaks. Season each generously with pepper (no salt) and brush with olive oil. Cook on the grill pan for 1 minute on each side. Lower the heat to medium and cook according to taste: 1½–2 minutes each side for rare; 2½–3 minutes each side for medium; 3–4 minutes on each side for well done.

Transfer the steaks to warmed individual plates and spoon the tomato and garlic sauce over them. Serve immediately.

SERVES 4–6

2 lb/900 g stewing beef, such as
  chuck or hind shank, trimmed
  and cut into 2-inch/5-cm chunks
2 onions, thinly sliced
2 carrots, thickly sliced
4 large garlic cloves, bruised
1 large bouquet garni
4 juniper berries
generous 2 cups full-bodied dry
  red wine, such as Fitou

2 tbsp brandy
2 tbsp olive oil
8 oz/225 g boned side of pork,
  rind removed
2 cups all-purpose flour
2 x 4-inch/10-cm strips of
  orange zest
3 oz/85 g black olives, pitted
  and rinsed to remove any brine
beef bouillon, if necessary
6 tbsp water
salt and pepper

TO GARNISH

fresh flatleaf parsley, chopped
orange zest, finely grated

freshly cooked pasta noodles, such
  as tagliatelle, to serve

BOEUF EN DAUBE À LA PROVENÇALE
beef stew with olives

Put the beef in a large, nonmetallic bowl and add the onions, carrots, garlic, bouquet garni, juniper berries, and seasoning. Pour over the wine, brandy, and oil, and stir. Cover with plastic wrap and marinate in the refrigerator for 24 hours. Remove the beef from the refrigerator 30 minutes before you plan to cook; preheat the oven to 325°F/160°C. Cut the pork into ¼-inch/5-mm strips. Add the pork to a pan of boiling water and blanch for 3 minutes, then drain. Remove the beef from the marinade and dry with paper towels. Put the beef and 3 tablespoons of the flour with salt and pepper in a plastic bag, close the top, and shake until it is coated. Remove from the bag, shake off excess flour, and set aside. Transfer half the pork to a 7-pint/3.4-liter flameproof casserole. Top with the beef and marinade, orange zest, and olives. Add the remaining pork. Top up with beef bouillon to cover the ingredients, if necessary.

Mix the remaining flour with the water to form a paste. Bring the casserole to a boil on top of the stove, then put the lid on and use your fingers to press the paste around the sides to seal. Transfer the casserole to the oven and cook for 1 hour. Lower the temperature to 275°F/140°C and cook for another 3 hours.

Remove the casserole from the oven and cut off the seal. Use a knife to insure the beef is tender. If not, re-cover and return to the oven; test again after 15 minutes. Using a metal spoon, skim any fat from the surface. Adjust the seasoning if necessary. Remove the bouquet garni, sprinkle the parsley and orange zest over the top, and serve with freshly cooked pasta noodles.

SERVES 6

2 tbsp olive oil

1 lb/450 g pearl onions, skinned
  (see Cook's Tip)

2 garlic cloves, halved

2 lb/900 g stewing beef, cubed

½ tsp ground cinnamon

1 tsp ground cloves

1 tsp ground cumin

2 tbsp tomato paste

1 bottle (generous 3 cups) full-bodied
  red wine

grated zest and juice of 1 orange

1 bay leaf

salt and pepper

fresh flatleaf parsley, chopped,
  to garnish

boiled or mashed potatoes, to serve

STIFÁDO
thick beef and pearl onion casserole

Heat the oil in a large, flameproof casserole. Add the whole onions and the garlic and cook for 5 minutes, or until softened and beginning to brown. Add the beef to the casserole and cook for about 5 minutes, stirring frequently, until browned on all sides.

Preheat the oven to 300°F/150°C. Stir the cinnamon, cloves, cumin, tomato paste, and salt and pepper into the casserole. Pour in the wine, stirring in any glazed bits from the bottom, then add the grated orange zest and the orange juice, and the bay leaf. Bring to a boil, then cover the casserole.

Cook in the preheated oven for about 1¼ hours. Remove the lid and cook the casserole for another hour, stirring once or twice during this time, until the meat is tender. Garnish with chopped fresh parsley and serve hot with boiled or mashed potatoes.

COOK'S TIP
If you find it difficult to skin the pearl onions, bring a large pan of water to a boil. Remove from the heat and plunge the onions quickly into the hot water, then into cold, before skinning.

SERVES 4

4 tbsp olive oil, plus extra for serving

3 oz/85 g pancetta or rindless sliced
   bacon, diced

1 onion, chopped

1 garlic clove, finely chopped

1 carrot, chopped

1 celery stalk, chopped

8 oz/225 g ground steak

4 oz/115 g chicken livers, chopped

2 tbsp strained tomatoes

½ cup dry white wine

scant 1 cup beef bouillon or water

1 tbsp chopped fresh oregano

1 bay leaf

1 lb/450 g dried tagliatelle

salt and pepper

Parmesan cheese, freshly grated,
   to serve

TAGLIATELLE ALLA BOLOGNESE
tagliatelle with a rich meat sauce

Heat the olive oil in a large, heavy-bottomed pot. Add the pancetta and cook over medium heat, stirring occasionally, for 3–5 minutes, or until it is just turning brown. Add the onion, garlic, carrot, and celery and cook, stirring occasionally, for another 5 minutes.

Add the steak and cook over high heat, breaking up the meat with a wooden spoon, for 5 minutes, or until browned. Stir in the chicken livers and cook, stirring occasionally, for another 2–3 minutes. Add the strained tomatoes, wine, bouillon, oregano, and bay leaf, and season to taste with salt and pepper. Bring to a boil, lower the heat, cover, and simmer for 30–35 minutes.

When the sauce is almost cooked, bring a large pan of lightly salted water to a boil. Add the pasta, bring back to a boil, and cook for 8–10 minutes, or until tender but still firm to the bite. Drain, transfer to a warmed serving dish, drizzle with a little olive oil, and toss well.

Remove the bay leaf from the sauce and discard, then pour the sauce over the pasta, toss again, and serve immediately with grated Parmesan.

SERVES 4

3 tbsp olive oil

1 onion, finely chopped

1 celery stalk, finely chopped

1 carrot, finely chopped

3½ oz/100 g pancetta or rindless sliced bacon, finely chopped

6 oz/175 g ground beef

6 oz/175 g ground pork

generous ⅓ cup dry red wine

1⅔ cup beef bouillon

1 tbsp tomato paste

1 clove

1 bay leaf

⅔ cup boiling milk

¼ cup unsalted butter, diced, plus extra for greasing

14 oz/400 g no-cook lasagna verdi

5 oz/140 g mozzarella cheese, drained and diced

¾ cup freshly grated Parmesan cheese

salt and pepper

BÉCHAMEL SAUCE

¼ cup unsalted butter

6 tbsp all-purpose flour

generous 2 cups milk

1 bay leaf

pinch of freshly grated nutmeg

salt and pepper

LASAGNE AL FORNO
lasagna

Heat the oil in a large pot, then add the onion, celery, carrot, pancetta, beef, and pork, and cook over medium heat, stirring frequently and breaking up the meat with a wooden spoon, for 10 minutes, or until browned.

Add the wine, bring to a boil, and cook until reduced. Add about two-thirds of the bouillon, bring to a boil, and cook until reduced. Combine the remaining bouillon and tomato paste and add to the pot. Season to taste, add the clove and the bay leaf, and pour in the milk. Cover and simmer over low heat for 1½ hours. Preheat the oven to 400°F/200°C. Lightly grease a large, ovenproof dish with butter.

To make the Béchamel Sauce, melt the butter in a pan, add the flour, and cook over low heat, stirring constantly, for 1 minute. Remove from the heat and stir in the milk. Return to the heat and bring to a boil, stirring constantly, until thickened and smooth. Add the bay leaf and simmer for 2 minutes. Remove the bay leaf; season with salt, pepper, and nutmeg. Remove from the heat.

Remove the meat sauce from the heat and discard the clove and bay leaf. Place a layer of lasagna in the bottom of the prepared ovenproof dish and cover it with a layer of meat sauce. Spoon a layer of Béchamel Sauce on top and sprinkle with one-third of the mozzarella and Parmesan cheeses. Continue making layers until all the ingredients are used, ending with a topping of Béchamel Sauce and sprinkled cheese. Dot the top of the lasagna with the diced butter and bake in the preheated oven for 30 minutes, or until golden and bubbling.

SERVES 4

4 pork loin steaks

2 tbsp olive oil

bunch of scallions, white parts only,
  thinly sliced

1 romaine lettuce, thinly sliced widthwise

1 tbsp chopped fresh dill

scant 1 cup chicken bouillon

2 eggs

juice of 1 large lemon

salt and pepper

HIRINÓ AVGOLÉMONO
pork and romaine lettuce in egg and lemon sauce

Season the pork steaks with pepper. Heat the oil in a large, heavy-bottomed skillet, add the scallions, and cook for 2 minutes, or until softened. Add the pork steaks and cook for 10 minutes, turning them several times, until browned on both sides and tender.

When the pork steaks are cooked, add the lettuce, dill, and bouillon to the skillet. Bring to a boil, cover, and then simmer for 4–5 minutes, or until the lettuce has wilted.

Meanwhile, put the eggs and lemon juice in a large bowl and whisk together.

Remove the pork steaks and lettuce from the pan with a slotted spoon, put in a warmed serving dish, and keep warm in a low oven. Strain the cooking liquid into a pitcher.

Gradually add 4 tablespoons of the hot cooking liquid to the lemon mixture, whisking all the time. Pour the egg mixture into the pan and simmer for 2–3 minutes, whisking all the time, until the sauce thickens. (Do not boil, or the sauce will curdle.) Season with salt and pepper. Ladle the sauce over the pork steaks and lettuce and serve hot.

SERVES 4–6

2 lb/900 g pork shoulder, boned and
    trimmed, but left in 1 piece

scant 1 cup dry white wine

6 garlic cloves, crushed

2 dried ancho or pasilla chilies

4 tbsp olive oil

2 large onions, chopped

4 red or green bell peppers, or a
    mixture, broiled, skinned, cored,
    seeded, and sliced

½ tsp hot paprika

1 lb 12 oz/800 g canned chopped
    tomatoes in their juice

2 sprigs fresh thyme

2 sprigs fresh parsley

salt and pepper

ESPALDA DE CERDO AL CHILINDRÓN
pork with bell peppers

Place the pork in a nonmetallic bowl. Pour over the wine and add 4 of the garlic cloves. Cover with plastic wrap and let marinate in the refrigerator for at least 8 hours.

Put the chilies in a heatproof bowl and pour over enough boiling water to cover. Let stand for 20 minutes to soften, then seed and chop. Set aside. Preheat the oven to 325°F/160°C.

Heat 4 tablespoons of oil in a large, heavy-bottomed flameproof casserole over medium-high heat. Add the onions and cook for 3 minutes, then add the remaining garlic cloves, chopped chilies, bell pepper slices, and paprika, and cook for another 2 minutes, or until the onions are soft but not brown. Use a slotted spoon to transfer the mixture to a plate.

Drain the pork, reserving the marinade, and pat dry. Add the pork to the casserole and cook until brown on both sides. Return the onion mixture to the casserole with the pork and stir in the marinade, tomatoes with their juices, and the herbs, then season to taste. Bring to a boil, scraping any glazed bits from the bottom of the pan. Transfer the casserole to the oven, and cook for 1 hour, or until the pork is tender.

If the juices are too thin, remove the pork from the casserole and keep warm. Put the casserole over high heat and let the juices bubble until well reduced. Taste and adjust the seasoning. Cut the pork into serving pieces and serve with the bell peppers and sauce from the casserole.

SERVES 6

3 lb 8 oz/1.6 kg loin of pork, boned
   and rolled

4 garlic cloves, thinly sliced lengthwise

1½ tsp finely chopped fresh fennel
   fronds or ½ tsp dried fennel

4 cloves

1¼ cups dry white wine

1¼ cups water

salt and pepper

ARROSTO ALLA PERUGINA
slow-roasted pork

Preheat the oven to 300°F/150°C. Use a small, sharp knife to make incisions all over the pork, opening them out slightly to make little pockets. Place the garlic slices in a small strainer and rinse under cold running water to moisten. Spread out the fennel on a saucer and roll the garlic slices in it to coat. Slide the garlic slices and the cloves into the pockets in the pork. Season the meat all over with salt and pepper.

Place the pork in a large ovenproof dish or roasting pan. Pour in the wine and water. Cook in the oven, basting the meat occasionally, for 2½–2¾ hours, or until the pork is tender but still moist.

If you are serving the pork hot, transfer it to a cutting board and cut into slices. If you are serving it cold, let it cool completely in the cooking juices before removing and slicing.

COOK'S TIP
Ready-prepared boned and rolled loin of pork is available from supermarkets and butchers, or you can ask your butcher to prepare one for you.

SERVES 4

1 lb/450 g pork tenderloin

2–3 tbsp extra-virgin olive oil

2 tbsp Sambuca

1 large fennel bulb, sliced, fronds
    reserved for garnish

3 oz/85 g Gorgonzola cheese, crumbled

2 tbsp light cream

1 tbsp chopped fresh sage

1 tbsp chopped fresh thyme

salt and pepper

SCALOPPINE DI MAIALE
CON FINOCCHIO

pork tenderloin with fennel

Trim any fat from the pork and cut into ¼-inch/5-mm slices. Place the slices between 2 sheets of plastic wrap and beat gently with the flat end of a meat pounder or with a rolling pin to flatten slightly.

Heat 2 tablespoons of the oil in a heavy-bottomed skillet and add the pork, in batches. Cook over medium heat for 2–3 minutes on each side, until tender. Remove from the pan and keep warm. Cook the remaining batches, adding more oil if necessary.

Stir the Sambuca into the pan, increase the heat, and cook, stirring constantly and scraping up the glazed bits from the bottom. Add the fennel and cook, stirring and turning frequently, for 3 minutes. Remove from the pan and keep warm.

Lower the heat, add the Gorgonzola and cream, and cook, stirring constantly, until smooth. Remove the pan from the heat, stir in the sage and thyme, and season to taste with salt and pepper.

Divide the pork among 4 warmed individual serving plates. Top with the fennel and pour over the sauce. Garnish with the reserved fennel fronds and serve immediately.

SERVES 4

4¼ cups chicken bouillon or vegetable bouillon

6 tbsp unsalted butter

3 shallots, finely chopped

4 oz/115 g pancetta or rindless sliced bacon, diced

scant 1½ cups arborio rice

⅔ cup dry white wine

1½ cups baby peas, thawed if frozen

salt and pepper

Parmesan cheese shavings, to garnish

92

RISI E BISI
rice and peas

Pour the bouillon into a large pan and bring to a boil. Lower the heat and simmer gently.

Melt 4 tablespoons of the butter in another large, heavy-bottomed pot. Add the shallots and pancetta and cook over low heat, stirring occasionally, for 5 minutes, or until the shallots are softened. Add the rice and cook, stirring constantly, for 2–3 minutes, or until all the grains are thoroughly coated and glistening.

Pour in the wine and cook, stirring constantly, until it has almost completely evaporated. Add a ladleful of hot bouillon and cook, stirring constantly, until all the bouillon has been absorbed. Continue cooking and adding the bouillon, a ladleful at a time, for about 10 minutes.

Add the peas, then continue adding the bouillon, a ladleful at a time, for another 10 minutes, or until the rice is tender and the liquid has been absorbed.

Stir in the remaining butter and season to taste with salt and pepper. Transfer the risotto to a warmed serving dish, garnish with Parmesan shavings, and serve immediately.

VARIATION
You can substitute diced cooked cured ham for the pancetta or bacon and add it toward the end of the cooking time so that it heats through.

Fish and Seafood

SERVES 4

about 2 tbsp all-purpose flour

4 hake fillets, about 5½ oz/150 g each

4 tbsp extra-virgin olive oil

½ cup dry white wine, such as a
  white Rioja

2 large garlic cloves, very
  finely chopped

6 scallions, thinly sliced

scant ½ cup very finely chopped
  fresh parsley

salt and pepper

MERLUZA A LA VASCA
hake in white wine

Preheat the oven to 450°F/230°C. Season the flour generously with salt and pepper on a flat plate. Dredge the skin side of the hake fillets in the seasoned flour, then shake off the excess. Set aside.

Heat a shallow, flameproof casserole over high heat until you can feel the heat rising. Add the oil and heat to 350–375°F/180–190°C, or until a cube of day-old bread browns in 30 seconds. Add the hake fillets, skin-side down and cook for 3 minutes, or until the skin is golden brown.

Turn the fish over and season with salt and pepper to taste. Pour in the wine and add the garlic, scallions, and parsley. Transfer the casserole to the preheated oven, uncovered, and bake for 5 minutes, or until the flesh flakes easily. Serve the meal straight from the casserole.

VARIATION
When hake isn't available, substitute with the same quantity of cod.

SERVES 4

2 skate wings

2 tbsp olive oil

1 onion, finely chopped

1 garlic clove, finely chopped

⅔ cups strained plain yogurt

1 tsp lemon juice

1 tbsp chopped fresh flatleaf parsley,
  plus extra to garnish

1 tbsp capers, coarsely chopped

1 tbsp whole-grain mustard

salt and pepper

lemon wedges, to serve

PSÁRI ME MOUSTÁRDA KAI CÁPARI

skate in mustard and caper sauce

Cut each skate wing in half and place in a large skillet. Cover with lightly salted water, bring to a boil, then simmer for 10–15 minutes, or until tender.

Meanwhile, make the mustard and caper sauce. Heat the oil in a pan, add the onion and garlic, and cook for 5 minutes, or until softened. Add the yogurt, lemon juice, parsley, and capers and cook for 1–2 minutes, or until heated through. (Do not boil, or the sauce will curdle.) Stir in the mustard and season with salt and pepper.

Drain the skate and put on 4 warmed serving plates. Pour over the mustard and caper sauce and sprinkle with chopped parsley. Serve hot with lemon wedges.

SERVES 4

2 lb/900 g salt

generous 1⅓ cups all-purpose flour

scant 1 cup water

2 lemon slices

few sprigs of fresh parsley

1 dorada, porgy, or red snapper, about
  2 lb 4 oz/1 kg, gutted through the gills

DORADA A LA SAL
fish baked in salt

Preheat the oven to 450°F/230°C. Mix the salt and flour in a bowl and make a well in the middle. Pour in the water to make a thick paste. Set the mixture aside.

Push the lemon and parsley into the gill cavity of the fish. Use paper towels to wipe the fish dry. Cover the fish with the salt paste, using your hands. (It's not necessary to scale the fish before you add the paste, but do take care not to cut yourself.) Place in a roasting pan, making sure the fish is completely covered.

Roast the fish in the preheated oven for 30 minutes. Remove from the oven and crack the crust. As you pull the crust back, it should bring the skin with it. Fillet the flesh and serve immediately.

COOK'S TIP
Gutting the fish through the gills keeps it in one piece, retaining both moisture and flavor. A fish dealer will do this for you, but with practice it can be done at home. Push back the flap over the gills and use your fingers to pull them out: be careful because they are sharp. Put your little finger into the cavity and use it to "hook" the innards, then pull them out in one swift movement. Use a teaspoon to scrape out anything left behind. Rinse the fish inside and out under cold water, then pat dry with paper towels.

SERVES 4

3 tbsp olive oil

1 tbsp all-purpose flour

4 cod fillets, about 6 oz/175 g each,
   skin removed and patted dry

1 large onion, finely chopped

4 large tomatoes, skinned, seeded,
   and chopped

2 large garlic cloves, crushed

⅔ cup dry white wine

½ tsp paprika, to taste

2 red bell peppers, broiled, skinned,
   cored, seeded, and cut into strips

2 green bell peppers, broiled, skinned,
   cored, seeded, and cut into strips

zest of 1 lemon, cut into broad strips

salt and pepper

fresh flatleaf parsley, finely chopped,
   to garnish

102 CABILLAUD À LA BASQUAISE
basque-style cod

Preheat the oven to 400°F/200°C. Heat 1 tablespoon of the oil in a flameproof casserole over medium-high heat. Season the flour with salt and pepper, then very lightly dust 1 side of each cod fillet with the flour. Cook, floured-side down, for 2 minutes, or until just golden. Set aside.

Wipe out the casserole, then heat the remaining oil over medium-high heat. Add the onion and sauté for 5 minutes, or until soft but not browned.

Stir in the tomatoes, garlic, wine, paprika, and salt and pepper to taste and bring to a boil. Lower the heat and simmer for 5 minutes, stirring occasionally.

Stir the red and green bell peppers into the casserole with the strips of lemon zest and bring to a boil. Lay the cod fillets on top, browned-side up, and season to taste with salt and pepper. Cover the casserole and bake for 12–15 minutes, depending on the thickness of the cod, until it is cooked through and flakes easily.

Discard the lemon zest just before serving. Serve the cod on a bed of the vegetables and sprinkle with the chopped parsley.

VARIATION
Hake is similar to cod and less expensive; it is also ideal to use in this dish.

SERVES 4

4 cod fillets, each about 6 oz/175 g

olive oil, for brushing

salt and pepper

lemon wedges, to serve

CATALAN SPINACH

generous ⅓ cup raisins

½ cup pine nuts

4 tbsp extra-virgin olive oil

3 garlic cloves, crushed

1 lb 2 oz/500 g baby spinach
    leaves, rinsed

104 BACALAO A LA CATALANA
cod with spinach

For the Catalan Spinach, put the raisins in a small bowl, cover with hot water, and set aside to soak for 15 minutes, then drain well.

Meanwhile, put the pine nuts in a skillet over medium-high heat and dry-cook for 1–2 minutes, shaking frequently, until toasted and golden brown: watch closely because they burn quickly.

Heat the oil in a large, lidded skillet over medium-high heat. Add the garlic and cook for 2 minutes, or until golden but not brown. Remove with a slotted spoon and discard.

Add the spinach to the oil with only the rinsing water that clings to its leaves. Cover and cook for 4–5 minutes, or until wilted. Uncover, stir in the drained raisins and the pine nuts, and continue cooking until all the liquid evaporates. Season to taste and keep warm.

To cook the cod, brush the fillets lightly with oil and sprinkle with salt and pepper. Place under a preheated hot broiler about 4 inches/10 cm from the heat and broil for 8–10 minutes, or until the flesh is opaque and flakes easily.

Divide the Catalan Spinach among 4 plates and place the cod fillets on top. Serve with lemon wedges.

SERVES 4

1 lb 5 oz/600 g angler fish fillet
1 green bell pepper
1 onion
3 tbsp olive oil
3 tbsp lemon juice

2 garlic cloves, crushed
16 large raw shrimp
16 fresh bay leaves
salt and pepper
lemon wedges, to garnish

SOUVLÁKIA ME PSÁRI KAI GARÍDES
angler fish and shrimp kabobs

Cut the angler fish into chunks measuring about 1 inch/2.5 cm. Cut the bell pepper into similar-size chunks, discarding the core and seeds. Cut the onion into 6 wedges, then cut each wedge in half widthwise and separate the layers.

To make the marinade, put the oil, lemon juice, garlic, and salt and pepper in a bowl, and whisk together. Add the angler fish, shrimp, onion, and bell pepper pieces, and toss together until coated in the marinade. Cover with plastic wrap and let marinate in the refrigerator for 2–3 hours.

Thread the pieces of fish, bell pepper, and onion, and the bay leaves onto 8 greased, flat, metal kabob skewers, alternating and dividing the ingredients as evenly as possible. Place on a greased broiler pan.

Preheat the broiler, then cook the kabobs under the broiler for 10–15 minutes, turning frequently and basting with any remaining marinade, until cooked and lightly charred. Serve hot, garnished with lemon wedges.

COOK'S TIP
These kabobs are ideal for cooking over a barbecue grill and eating outdoors. Light a charcoal barbecue grill 45 minutes before starting to cook (or 10 minutes if using a gas barbecue grill) and start cooking when the flames die down and the coals are glowing red. Cook for the same time under a broiler.

SERVES 4

6 red snapper fillets, about 4½ oz/125 g each, scaled

4 tbsp olive oil

2 large red bell peppers, cored, seeded and thinly sliced

2 fennel bulbs, thinly sliced

2 large garlic cloves, crushed

salt and pepper

lemon wedges, to serve

ROUGET GRILLÉ AUX POIVRONS ET FENOUIL

broiled red snapper with fennel and bell peppers

Pick over the red snapper fillets and use a pair of tweezers to remove the fine bones running along the center of each fillets.

Heat 2 tablespoons of the oil in a large sauté pan or skillet with a lid over medium-high heat. Add the bell peppers, fennel, and garlic, and stir. Season, then lower the heat to medium-low, cover the pan, and let the vegetables cook for 15–20 minutes, or until soft.

Meanwhile, preheat the broiler to high. When the broiler is very, very hot, brush the skin of the fillets with oil and season to taste with salt and pepper. Put the fillets on a cookie sheet, skin-sides up, and broil for 3 minutes, or until the skin crisps and becomes golden brown. Turn the fillets over, brush again with oil, and season to taste. Continue to broil for a minute or so, until the flesh flakes easily when tested with the tip of a knife.

Divide the fennel and bell peppers among 4 plates. Cut each fillet in half and arrange 3 pieces on top of each portion of the vegetables. Serve immediately with lemon wedges.

SERVES 4

8 small, fresh grape leaves or one 8-oz/
225-g package grape leaves preserved
in brine

4 red snapper, each about 7 oz/200 g,
scaled and gutted

1 lemon, thinly sliced, then halved

small bunch of fresh dill

2 tbsp olive oil

salt and pepper

BARBOÚNIA ME AMBELÓFILA
red snapper wrapped in grape leaves

If using fresh grape leaves, tie them in bundles by their stalks, and blanch them in boiling salted water for 1 minute. Rinse under cold running water, dry the leaves, and cut out the stalks. If using preserved grape leaves, place them in a large bowl, pour over boiling water, and let soak for 20 minutes. Drain, soak in cold water for 20 minutes, and then drain again.

Season the fish cavities with salt and pepper, then insert some halved lemon slices and 2–3 sprigs of fresh dill in each. Brush the fish with the olive oil and season with salt and pepper.

Preheat the broiler. Place 1 fish on 2 fresh, overlapping grape leaves or on 5–6 preserved grape leaves. Roll up the fish and, if using fresh grape leaves, tie with kitchen string.

Cook the fish under the broiler for 10 minutes, or until tender. Serve hot.

SERVES 4

generous 4 cups dry, white bread crumbs

2 tbsp milk

1 fennel bulb, thinly sliced, fronds reserved for garnish

1 tbsp lemon juice

2 tbsp Sambuca

1 tbsp chopped fresh thyme

1 bay leaf, crumbled

3 lb 5 oz/1.5 kg whole porgy, cleaned, scaled, and boned

3 tbsp olive oil, plus extra for brushing

1 red onion, chopped

1¼ cups dry white wine

salt and pepper

lemon wedges, to serve

FRAGOLINO AL FORNO
roast porgy with fennel

Preheat the oven to 475°F/240°C. Place the bread crumbs in a bowl, add the milk, and set aside for 5 minutes to soak. Place the fennel in another bowl and add the lemon juice, Sambuca, thyme, and bay leaf. Squeeze the bread crumbs and add them to the mixture, stirring well.

Rinse the fish inside and out under cold running water and pat dry with paper towels. Season with salt and pepper. Spoon the fennel mixture into the cavity, then bind the fish with trussing thread or kitchen string.

Brush a large ovenproof pan with olive oil and sprinkle the onion over the bottom. Lay the fish on top and pour in the wine—it should reach about one-third of the way up the fish. Drizzle the porgy with the olive oil and cook in the preheated oven for 25–30 minutes. Baste the fish occasionally with the cooking juices and, if it begins to brown, cover with a piece of foil to protect it.

Carefully lift out the fish, remove the string, and place on a warmed serving platter. Garnish with the reserved fennel fronds and serve immediately with lemon wedges.

SERVES 4–6

5 tbsp olive oil

2 onions, thinly sliced

2 garlic cloves, finely chopped

2 carrots, thinly sliced

2 celery stalks, thinly sliced

⅔ cup dry white wine

14 oz/400 g canned chopped tomatoes
   in their juice

pinch of sugar

1 large lemon, thinly sliced

2 tbsp chopped fresh flatleaf parsley

1 tsp chopped fresh marjoram

2¼–3 lb/1–1.3 kg fat whole fish, such
   as porgy, bass, tilapia, or red snapper,
   scaled and gutted

salt and pepper

PSÁRI PLAKÍ
traditional greek baked fish

Preheat the oven to 350°F/180°C. Heat 4 tablespoons of the oil in a large pan, add the onions and garlic, and cook for 5 minutes, or until softened. Add the carrots and celery and cook for 5–10 minutes, or until slightly softened.

Pour the wine into the pan and bring to a boil. Add the tomatoes and their juice, the sugar, lemon slices, and salt and pepper, and simmer for 20 minutes. Add the parsley and marjoram.

Put the fish in a greased, shallow, ovenproof pan. Arrange the vegetables around the fish, scattering some of the lemon slices on top. Sprinkle with the remaining oil and season with salt and pepper.

Bake the fish, uncovered, in the preheated oven for 45 minutes–1 hour depending on the thickness of the fish, until tender. Serve immediately, straight from the oven.

SERVES 4

4 fresh tuna steaks, about ¾ inch/
  2 cm thick

olive oil, for brushing

salt and pepper

GREEN SAUCE

1 cup fresh flatleaf parsley, leaves
  and stems

4 scallions, chopped

2 garlic cloves, chopped

3 anchovy fillets in oil, drained

scant ½ cup fresh basil leaves

½ tbsp capers in brine, rinsed and dried

2 sprigs of fresh oregano or ½ tsp
  dried oregano

½ cup extra-virgin olive oil, plus extra
  if necessary

1–2 tbsp lemon juice, to taste

THON SAUCE VERTE
tuna with green sauce

To make the Green Sauce, put the parsley, scallions, garlic, anchovy fillets, basil, capers, and oregano in a food processor. Pulse to chop and blend together. With the motor still running, pour in the oil through the feed tube. Add lemon juice to taste, then whizz again. If the sauce is too thick, add a little extra oil. Transfer to a bowl, cover with plastic wrap, and chill until required.

Place a ridged cast-iron skillet over high heat until you can feel the heat rising from the surface. Brush the tuna steaks with oil, place them oiled-sides down on the hot pan, and cook for 2 minutes.

Lightly brush the top sides of the tuna steaks with a little more oil. Use a pair of tongs to turn the tuna steaks over, then season to taste with salt and pepper. Continue cooking for another 2 minutes for rare or up to 4 minutes for well done.

Transfer the tuna steaks to serving plates and serve with the Green Sauce spooned over.

COOK'S TIP
The Green Sauce can be made up to a day in advance and chilled in a covered container in the refrigerator. Pour a thin layer of oil over the top of the sauce to preserve the color. The oil can be stirred in before serving.

SERVES 4–6

generous ¾ cup freshly squeezed
   orange juice
3 tbsp extra-virgin olive oil
2 oz/55 g anchovy fillets in oil, coarsely
   chopped, with the oil reserved

small pinch of dried chili flakes,
   or to taste
1 tuna fillet, about 1 lb 5 oz/600 g
pepper

ATÚN ASADO CON NARANJA Y ANCHOAS

roasted tuna with orange and anchovies

Combine the orange juice, 2 tablespoons of the olive oil, the anchovies and their oil, the chili, and black pepper to taste in a nonmetallic bowl. Add the tuna and spoon the marinade over it. Cover with plastic wrap and chill for at least 2 hours to marinate, turning the tuna occasionally. Remove the fish from the refrigerator 20 minutes before cooking.

Preheat the oven to 425°F/220°C. Remove the tuna from the marinade and wipe dry with paper towels. Reserve the marinade. Heat the remaining oil in a skillet over high heat. Add the tuna and sear for 1 minute on each side, until lightly browned and crisp. Place the tuna in a roasting pan and cover with foil.

Roast for 8 minutes for medium-rare and 10 minutes for medium-well done. Remove from the oven and set aside for at least 2 minutes before carving.

Meanwhile, put the marinade in a small pan over high heat and bring to a rolling boil for at least 2 minutes. Transfer the tuna to a serving platter and carve into thick slices, which will probably break into chunks as you cut them. Serve the sauce separately for spooning over. The tuna can be served hot or at room temperature, but the sauce is best served hot.

SERVES 4

8 oz/225 g raw shrimp

8 oz/225 g live mussels

8 oz/225 g live clams

2 garlic cloves, halved

1 lemon, sliced

2½ cups water

½ cup unsalted butter

1 tbsp olive oil

1 onion, finely chopped

2 tbsp chopped fresh flatleaf parsley

1¾ cups arborio rice

½ cup dry white wine

8 oz/225 g prepared squid, cut into
small pieces, or squid rings

4 tbsp Marsala

salt and pepper

RISOTTO ALLA MARINARA
seafood risotto

Peel the shrimp, reserving the heads and shells. Cut a slit along the back of each, remove and discard the dark vein, then reserve. Scrub the mussels and clams under cold running water and debeard the mussels, discarding any that are damaged or broken or those that do not shut immediately when tapped sharply. Wrap the shrimp heads and shells in a square of cheesecloth and pound gently with a pestle, reserving any liquid.

Place the garlic, lemon, mussels, and clams in a large pan, and add the wrapped shells and any reserved liquid. Pour in the water, cover tightly, and bring to a boil over high heat. Cook, shaking the pan frequently, for 5 minutes, or until the shellfish have opened. Discard any that remain closed. Transfer the mussels and clams to a bowl and strain the cooking liquid through a cheesecloth-lined strainer into a pitcher, adding water to make up to 5 cups. Pour into a clean pan. Bring to a boil, then lower the heat and simmer gently.

Melt 2 tablespoons of the butter with the oil in a pan. Add the onion and half the parsley and cook over low heat, stirring occasionally, for 5 minutes, until softened. Add the rice and cook, stirring constantly, for 2–3 minutes, until the grains are coated. Add the wine and cook, stirring constantly, until it has almost completely evaporated. Add a ladleful of the bouillon and cook, stirring, until it has been absorbed. Continue cooking, stirring, and adding the bouillon, a ladleful at a time, for 20 minutes, or until the rice is tender and the liquid has been absorbed. About 5 minutes before the rice is ready, melt ¼ cup of the remaining butter in a pan. Add the squid and cook, stirring frequently, for 3 minutes, then add the reserved shrimp and cook for another 2–3 minutes, or until the squid is opaque and the shrimp have changed color. Stir in the Marsala, bring to a boil, and cook until the liquid has evaporated. Stir the seafood into the rice, add the remaining butter and parsley, and season. Heat through briefly and serve.

SERVES 4

20 large, fresh scallops, removed
    from their shells, about 1½ inches/
    4 cm thick

⅞ cup clarified butter

3 oz/85 g day-old French bread or
    other crusty bread, made into fine
    bread crumbs

4 garlic cloves, finely chopped

5 tbsp finely chopped fresh
    flatleaf parsley

lemon wedges, to serve

COQUILLES ST JACQUES À LA PROVENÇALE
scallops with bread crumbs and parsley

Preheat the oven to its lowest temperature. Use a small knife to remove the dark vein that runs around each scallop, then rinse and pat dry. Season to taste with salt and pepper and set aside.

Melt half the butter in a large sauté pan or skillet over high heat. Add the bread crumbs, lower the heat to medium, and cook, stirring, for 5–6 minutes, or until they are golden-brown and crisp. Remove the bread crumbs from the pan and drain well on paper towels, then keep warm in the oven. Wipe out the pan.

For the next stage, it is best to use 2 large sauté pans or skillets to cook all the scallops at once without overcrowding the pans. Melt scant ¼ cup of the butter in each pan over high heat. Lower the heat to medium, divide the scallops and garlic between the 2 pans in single layers, and cook for 2 minutes.

Turn the scallops over and cook for another 2–3 minutes, or until they are golden and cooked through—cut one with a knife to check. Add extra butter to the pans if necessary.

Divide the scallops among 4 warmed plates and sprinkle with the bread crumbs and parsley mixed together. Serve with lemon wedges for squeezing over.

SERVES 2

PIZZA DOUGH

2¼ cups all-purpose flour, plus
  extra for dusting

1 tsp salt

1 tsp rapid-rise dry yeast

1 tbsp olive oil, plus extra for
  brushing and drizzling

6 tbsp lukewarm water

TOMATO SAUCE

8 oz/225 g plum tomatoes

2 tbsp olive oil

1 small onion, finely chopped

1 garlic clove, finely chopped

1 red bell pepper, cored, seeded
  and chopped

1 tbsp tomato paste

1 tsp soft brown sugar

1 tbsp shredded fresh basil leaves

1 bay leaf

TOPPING

8 oz/225 g mixed fresh seafood,
  including cooked shrimp,
  cooked mussels, and squid rings

½ red and ½ yellow bell pepper,
  cored, seeded and chopped

1 tbsp capers, rinsed

generous ½ cup grated Taleggio
  cheese (if unavailable, use
  mozzarella instead)

3 tbsp freshly grated
  Parmesan cheese

½ tsp dried oregano

2¾ oz/75 g anchovy fillets in oil,
  drained and sliced

10 black olives, pitted

salt and pepper

PIZZA ALLA MARINARA
seafood pizza

To make the Pizza Dough, sift the flour and salt into a bowl and stir in the yeast.
Make a well in the center and pour in the oil and water. Gradually incorporate the
dry ingredients into the liquid, using a wooden spoon or floured hands. Turn out the
dough onto a lightly floured counter and knead well for 5 minutes, or until smooth
and elastic. Return to the clean bowl, cover with lightly oiled plastic wrap, and set
aside to rise in a warm place for 1 hour, or until doubled in size.

To make the Tomato Sauce, remove the stems and cut a small cross in the top of each
tomato. Put the tomatoes into a heatproof bowl, pour over enough boiling water to
cover, and let stand for 30 seconds. Use a slotted spoon to transfer to a bowl of ice
water. Working with 1 tomato at a time, remove the skin, then cut in half, and use a
teaspoon to scoop out the cores and seeds. Heat the olive oil in a heavy-bottomed pan.
Add the onion, garlic, and bell pepper and cook over low heat, stirring occasionally,
for 5 minutes, until softened. Add the tomatoes, tomato paste, sugar, basil, and bay
leaf and season to taste with salt and pepper. Cover and simmer, stirring occasionally,
for 30 minutes, until thickened. Remove the pan from the heat and set aside to cool.

Preheat the oven to 425°F/220°C. Turn out the pizza dough onto a lightly floured
counter and punch down. Knead briefly, then roll out the dough into a circle about
¼ inch/5 mm thick. Transfer to a lightly oiled cookie sheet and push up the edge with
your fingers to form a small rim. Spread the sauce over the pizza dough, almost to
the edge. Arrange the Topping ingredients over the pizza, drizzle with olive oil, and
season to taste with salt and pepper. Bake in the preheated oven for 20–25 minutes,
or until the crust is crisp and the cheese has melted. Serve immediately.

SERVES 4

8 sun-dried tomatoes

8 small prepared squid (bodies about
    5 inches/13 cm long)

scant 1½ cups fresh white
    bread crumbs

2 tbsp capers, rinsed and finely chopped

2 tbsp chopped fresh flatleaf parsley

1 egg white

olive oil, for brushing and drizzling

3 tbsp dry white wine

salt and pepper

lemon juice, for drizzling (optional)

CALAMARI RIPIENI
stuffed squid

Put the sun-dried tomatoes in a bowl and cover with boiling water. Set aside for 15–20 minutes.

Meanwhile, finely chop the squid tentacles and place in another bowl. Reserve the body sacs. Add the bread crumbs, capers, and parsley. Preheat the oven to 325°F/160°C.

Thoroughly drain the tomatoes and pat dry with paper towels. Chop them finely and add to the bread crumb mixture. Mix thoroughly and season to taste with salt and pepper. Stir in the egg white.

Spoon the bread crumb mixture into the squid body sacs, pushing it down well. Do not fill them more than about three-fourths full, or they will burst during cooking. Secure the opening of each sac with a toothpick so the stuffing will not ooze out.

Generously brush oil over an ovenproof dish large enough to hold the squid snugly in a single layer. Place the squid in the dish and pour in the wine. Cover with foil and bake in the preheated oven for about 45 minutes, turning and basting occasionally. Test with a fork to check if the squid is tender.

Remove from the oven and set aside to cool to room temperature. To serve, remove and discard the toothpicks and slice the squid into circles. Place on warmed individual plates and drizzle with a little olive oil and either the cooled cooking juices or lemon juice.

SERVES 3

2 tbsp unsalted butter

1 tbsp olive oil

1 onion, very finely chopped

6 oz/175 g zucchini, halved lengthwise
  and sliced

1 celery stalk, very finely chopped

3 oz/85 g white mushrooms, sliced

2 oz/55 g green beans, cut into
  2-inch/5-cm lengths

4 eggs

⅓ cup mascarpone cheese

1 tbsp chopped fresh thyme

1 tbsp shredded fresh basil

7 oz/200 g canned tuna, drained
  and flaked

4 oz/115 g cooked peeled shrimp

salt and pepper

128 FRITTATA DI FRUTTI DI MARE
seafood omelet

Melt the butter with the olive oil in a heavy-bottomed skillet with a flameproof handle. If the skillet has a wooden handle, protect it with foil because it needs to go under the broiler. Add the onion and cook over low heat, stirring occasionally, for 5 minutes, or until softened.

Add the zucchini, celery, mushrooms, and beans, and cook, stirring occasionally, for another 8–10 minutes, or until beginning to brown.

Beat the eggs with the mascarpone, thyme, and basil, and salt and pepper to taste. Preheat the broiler to hot.

Add the tuna to the skillet and stir it into the mixture with a wooden spoon. Add the shrimp last.

Pour the egg mixture into the skillet and cook for 5 minutes, or until it is just beginning to set. Draw the egg from the sides of the pan toward the center to let the uncooked egg run underneath.

Put the pan under the preheated broiler and cook until the egg is just set and the surface is beginning to brown. Cut the frittata into wedges and serve.

SERVES 4

3 tbsp olive oil

1 onion, finely chopped

1 red bell pepper, cored, seeded, and
 thinly sliced

1 garlic clove, crushed

1¼ cup long-grain white rice

scant 3 cups fish, chicken, or
 vegetable bouillon

1 bay leaf

salt and pepper

14 oz/400 g cooked peeled shrimp,
 thawed and drained if frozen

TO GARNISH

whole cooked shrimp

lemon wedges

Greek black olives

TO SERVE

Kefalotiri or romano cheese, grated

cubes of Greek feta cheese

GARÍDES PILÁFI
shrimp pilaf

Heat the oil in a large, lidded skillet, add the onion, red bell pepper, and garlic, and cook for 5 minutes, or until softened. Add the rice and cook for 2–3 minutes, stirring all the time, until the grains look transparent.

Add the bouillon, bay leaf, and salt and pepper. Bring to a boil, cover the skillet with a tightly fitting lid, and simmer for 15 minutes, or until the rice is tender and the liquid has been absorbed. Do not stir during cooking. When cooked, very gently stir in the shrimp.

Remove the lid, cover the skillet with a clean dish towel, replace the lid, and let stand in a warm place for 10 minutes to dry out. Stir with a fork to separate the grains and serve garnished with whole shrimp, lemon wedges, and black olives. Accompany with Kefalotiri or romano cheese for sprinkling on top and a bowl of cubed feta cheese.

SERVES 4

2 lb 4 oz/1 kg live clams

¾ cup water

¾ cup dry white wine

12 oz/350 g spaghetti

5 tbsp olive oil

2 garlic cloves, finely chopped

4 tbsp chopped fresh flatleaf parsley

salt and pepper

SPAGHETTI ALLA VONGOLE
spaghetti with clams

Scrub the clams under cold running water and discard any with broken or damaged shells or those that do not shut when tapped sharply. Place the clams in a large, heavy-bottomed pot, add the water and wine, cover, and cook over high heat, shaking the pan occasionally, for 5 minutes, or until the shells have opened.

Remove the clams with a slotted spoon and set aside to cool slightly. Strain the cooking liquid through a cheesecloth-lined strainer into a small pan. Bring to a boil and cook until reduced by about half, then remove from the heat. Meanwhile, discard any clams that have not opened, remove the remainder from their shells, and set aside.

Bring a large pan of lightly salted water to a boil. Add the pasta, bring back to a boil, and cook for 8–10 minutes, or until tender but still firm to the bite.

Meanwhile, heat the olive oil in a large, heavy-bottomed skillet. Add the garlic and cook, stirring frequently, for 2 minutes. Add the parsley and the reduced cooking liquid and simmer gently.

Drain the pasta and add it to the skillet with the clams. Season to taste with salt and pepper and cook, stirring constantly, for 4 minutes, or until the pasta is coated and the clams have heated through. Transfer to a warmed serving dish and serve immediately.

COOK'S TIP
Do not be tempted to serve Parmesan for sprinkling: cheese does not partner well with this pasta recipe.

Vegetarian

SERVES 6

6 small red bell peppers

2 tbsp olive oil

3 garlic cloves, thinly sliced

9 oz/250 g halloumi cheese, thinly sliced

12 fresh mint leaves

grated zest and juice of 1 lemon

1 tbsp chopped fresh thyme

3 tbsp pine nuts

pepper

PIPÉRIES GEMISTÉS ME HALLÓUMI

roasted red bell peppers with halloumi

Preheat the oven to 400°F/200°C. Cut the bell peppers in half lengthwise and remove the cores and seeds. Leave the stems on. Rub the skins of the bell peppers with a little of the oil, then lightly oil a large cookie sheet, and arrange the bell peppers on it, skin-sides down.

Scatter half the garlic into the bell peppers. Add the cheese and then the mint leaves, lemon zest, remaining garlic, thyme, pine nuts, and pepper to taste. Drizzle over the remaining oil and the lemon juice.

Roast the bell peppers in the preheated oven for 30 minutes, or until tender and beginning to char around the edges. Serve warm.

SERVES 4

8 large cabbage leaves, such as napa cabbage or romaine lettuce

1 lb 12 oz/800 g canned tomatoes in their juice

2 tbsp olive oil

2 onions, finely chopped

1 large garlic clove, finely chopped

generous ¼ cup arborio or other short-grain rice

generous ⅓ cup golden raisins

1 tbsp chopped fresh mint

1¼ cups vegetable bouillon

1 tsp dried oregano

½ cup pine nuts

salt and pepper

LÁHANO DOLMÁDES
stuffed cabbage leaves

Plunge the cabbage into a large pan of boiling water, return to a boil, and then boil for 3–4 minutes, or until softened. Drain well, plunge into ice water, and then drain well again. If necessary, cut out any hard cores.

Take 3–4 of the canned tomatoes and chop into fairly small pieces. Heat 1 tablespoon of the oil in a pan. Add half the onions and all the garlic and cook for 5–10 minutes, or until softened and browned. Stir in the chopped tomatoes, and the rice, golden raisins, and mint.

Add the bouillon to the pan and bring to a boil, then simmer for 15–20 minutes, or until the rice is tender and the bouillon has been absorbed.

Meanwhile, make the tomato sauce. Heat the remaining oil in a pan, add the remaining onion, and cook for 5–10 minutes, or until softened and browned. Stir in the remaining canned tomatoes and their juice, with the oregano and salt and pepper, and bring to a boil, then simmer for about 10 minutes. Let cool slightly, then purée in a food processor or blender, or use a hand-held blender. Preheat the oven to 350°F/180°C.

When the rice is cooked, remove from the heat, stir in the pine nuts, and season with salt and pepper. Divide the stuffing mixture among the cabbage leaves and roll up and fold the leaves to form 8 neat packages. Place seam-sides down, side by side, in a shallow, ovenproof dish.

Pour the tomato sauce over the stuffed cabbage leaves. Cover the dish and bake in the preheated oven for 1 hour. Serve hot or warm.

SERVES 4

1 lb 5 oz/600 g eggplants, cut
  into ½-inch/1-cm slices

1 lb 5 oz/600 g plum tomatoes, cut into
  ½-inch/1-cm slices

scant 1 cup olive oil

⅓ cup freshly grated Parmesan cheese

2 tbsp fresh white bread crumbs

salt and pepper

MELANZANE E POMODORI AL FORNO

baked eggplants and tomatoes

To remove any bitterness, layer the eggplant slices in a colander, sprinkling each layer with salt. Let drain for 30 minutes. Meanwhile, spread out the tomato slices on paper towels, cover with more paper towels, and let drain.

Preheat the oven to 350°F/180°C. Rinse the eggplants thoroughly under cold running water to remove all traces of the salt, then pat dry with paper towels.

Heat 2 tablespoons of the olive oil in a skillet. Add the tomato slices and cook for 30 seconds on each side. Transfer to a platter and season to taste.

Wipe out the pan with paper towels, then add 2 tablespoons of the remaining oil and heat. Add the eggplant slices, in batches, and cook on both sides, until golden brown. Remove from the pan and drain on paper towels. Cook the remaining slices in the same way, adding more oil as required.

Brush a large ovenproof dish with some of the remaining olive oil. Arrange alternate layers of eggplants and tomatoes, sprinkling each layer with Parmesan cheese. Top with the bread crumbs and drizzle with the remaining olive oil.

Bake in the preheated oven for 25–30 minutes, or until golden. Serve immediately.

VEGETARIAN

SERVES 4

4 fat, medium zucchini

3 tbsp olive oil

1 onion, finely chopped

1 garlic clove, finely chopped

generous ½ cup crumbled Greek
  feta cheese

¼ cup walnut pieces, chopped

1 cup fresh white bread crumbs

1 egg, beaten

1 tsp chopped fresh dill

salt and pepper

KOLOKÍTHIA GEMISTÁ
stuffed zucchini with walnuts and feta

Preheat the oven to 375°F/190°C. Put the zucchini in a pan of boiling water, return to a boil, and then boil for 3 minutes. Drain, rinse under cold water, and drain again. Let cool.

When the zucchini are cool enough to handle, cut a thin strip off the top side of each one with a sharp knife, and gently score around the inside edges to help scoop out the flesh. Using a teaspoon, scoop out the flesh, leaving a shell to hold the stuffing. Chop the zucchini flesh.

Heat 2 tablespoons of the oil in a pan. Add the onion and garlic and cook for 5 minutes, or until softened. Add the zucchini flesh and cook for 5 minutes, or until the onion is golden brown. Remove from the heat and let cool slightly. Stir in the cheese and then the walnuts, bread crumbs, egg, dill, and salt and pepper. Use the stuffing to fill the zucchini shells and place side by side in an ovenproof dish. Drizzle over the remaining oil.

Cover the dish with foil and bake in the preheated oven for 30 minutes. Remove the foil and bake for another 10–15 minutes, or until golden brown. Serve hot.

SERVES 4

4 large, long, thin eggplants

scant 1 cup olive oil

3 large onions, thinly sliced

2 large garlic cloves, finely chopped

1 green bell pepper, cored, seeded, and
   thinly sliced

14 oz/400 g canned tomatoes, drained

1 tsp dried oregano

¼ tsp dried thyme

4 tbsp chopped fresh flatleaf
   parsley, plus extra to garnish

2 tbsp lemon juice

salt and pepper

MELITZÁNES GÉMISTES
baked stuffed eggplants

Cut the eggplants in half lengthwise. Scoop out the flesh, leaving a shell to hold the stuffing. Sprinkle the insides with salt, place upside-down on a plate, and reserve. Coarsely chop the scooped-out flesh and place in a colander, stand it over a large plate, and sprinkle each layer with salt. Cover with a plate and place a heavy weight on top. Leave both the shells and flesh for 30 minutes to degorge.

Rinse the eggplant shells and chopped flesh under cold running water, then pat dry with paper towels. Heat 4 tablespoons of the olive oil in a pan. Add the onions, garlic, and green bell pepper, and cook for 10–15 minutes, or until softened, stirring occasionally.

Add the eggplant flesh, then the tomatoes, breaking them up with a fork, then the oregano, thyme, parsley, and salt and pepper. Simmer for 20–30 minutes, or until the mixture has reduced and thickened slightly. Preheat the oven to 300°F/150°C.

Preheat the oven to 300°F/150°C. Spoon the stuffing into the eggplant shells and place them, side by side, in a shallow, ovenproof dish.

Pour the remaining oil around the eggplants. Add the lemon juice and enough boiling water to come halfway up the sides of the eggplants. Cover the dish with foil and cook in the preheated oven for 1 hour, or until tender. Let cool in the liquid, but do not chill.

To serve, lift out the eggplants with a slotted spoon, discard the liquid, and garnish with chopped parsley.

SERVES 4–6

5 tbsp olive oil

2 large onions, thinly sliced

4 large garlic cloves, finely chopped

12 oz/350 g eggplants, coarsely chopped

12 oz/350 g zucchini, sliced

4 large beefsteak tomatoes, skinned, seeded, and chopped

1 large bouquet garni of 2 large sprigs of fresh flatleaf parsley, 2 sprigs of fresh thyme, and 2 sprigs of fresh basil, tied together to a piece of celery

½ tsp sugar

salt and pepper

fresh basil leaves, to garnish

RATATOUILLE
ratatouille

Heat the oil in a large, flameproof casserole over medium heat. Add the onions and stir for 3 minutes. Add the garlic and stir around for another 3 minutes, or until the onions are soft but not brown.

Stir in the eggplants, zucchini, tomatoes, bouquet garni, and sugar, and salt and pepper to taste. Reduce the heat to low, cover the casserole tightly, and simmer for 45 minutes, without lifting the lid for at least the first 15 minutes.

Taste, and adjust the seasoning if necessary. Sprinkle with the basil leaves and serve immediately or let cool.

COOK'S TIP
Leftover Ratatouille makes a simple supper wrapped inside crêpes.

SERVES 4

generous ⅓ cup butter, plus extra
  for greasing
12 oz/350 g mixed exotic mushrooms,
  sliced
12 oz/350 g dried tagliatelle
2 egg yolks
4 tbsp freshly grated romano cheese
salt and pepper

BÉCHAMEL SAUCE

¼ cup unsalted butter
½ cup all-purpose flour
generous 2 cups milk
1 bay leaf
generous 1⅓ cups thinly sliced
  fontina cheese
pinch of freshly grated nutmeg
salt and pepper

CROSTATA AI FUNGHI
baked pasta with mushrooms

Melt 2 tablespoons of the butter in a large pan. Add the mushrooms and cook over low heat, stirring occasionally, for 10 minutes. Preheat the oven to 400°F/200°C.

To make the Béchamel Sauce, melt the butter in a pan, add the flour, and cook over low heat, stirring constantly, for 1 minute. Remove from the heat and gradually stir in the milk. Return to the heat and bring to a boil, stirring constantly, until thickened and smooth. Add the bay leaf and simmer for 2 minutes. Remove the bay leaf, add the fontina cheese, and season with salt, pepper, and nutmeg. Remove from the heat.

Meanwhile, bring a large pan of lightly salted water to a boil. Add the pasta, bring back to a boil, and cook for 8–10 minutes, or until tender but still firm to the bite. Drain, return to the pan, and add the remaining butter, the egg yolks and about one-third of the sauce, then season to taste with salt and pepper. Toss well to mix, then gently stir in the mushrooms.

Lightly grease a large, ovenproof dish and spoon in the pasta mixture. Pour over the remaining sauce evenly and sprinkle with the grated romano cheese.

Bake in the preheated oven for 15–20 minutes, or until golden brown. Serve immediately.

SERVES 4

⅔ cup dry white wine

1 tbsp sun-dried tomato paste

2 fresh red chilies

2 garlic cloves, finely chopped

12 oz/350 g dried tortiglioni (if unavailable, use other large pasta tubes instead)

4 tbsp chopped fresh flatleaf parsley

salt and pepper

shavings of romano cheese, to garnish

SUGOCASA

5 tbsp extra-virgin olive oil

1 lb/450 g plum tomatoes, chopped

salt and pepper

150 PASTA ALL'ARRABBIATA
hot chili pasta

First make the Sugocasa. Heat the olive oil in a skillet until it is almost smoking. Add the tomatoes and cook over high heat for 2–3 minutes. Lower the heat and cook gently for 20 minutes, or until very soft. Season with salt and pepper, then pass through a food mill into a clean pan.

Add the wine, tomato paste, whole chilies, and garlic to the Sugocasa and bring to a boil. Lower the heat and simmer gently.

Meanwhile, bring a large pan of lightly salted water to a boil. Add the pasta, bring back to a boil, and cook for 8–10 minutes, or until tender but still firm to the bite.

Meanwhile, remove the chilies and taste the sauce. If you prefer a hotter flavor, chop some or all of the chilies and return them to the pan. Check the seasoning at the same time, then stir in half of the parsley.

Drain the pasta and tip it into a warm serving bowl. Add the sauce and toss to coat. Sprinkle with the remaining parsley, garnish with the romano shavings, and serve immediately.

COOK'S TIP

If time is short, use ready-made Sugocasa, available from most supermarkets. It is sometimes labeled "crushed tomatoes." Failing that, you could use strained tomatoes, but the sauce will be thinner.

VEGETARIAN

SERVES 4

1 lb/450 g farfalle

2 tbsp unsalted butter

scant 1 cup heavy cream

pinch of freshly grated nutmeg

⅓ cup freshly grated Parmesan cheese,
    plus extra to serve

salt and pepper

sprigs of flat leaf parsley, to garnish

farfalle with cream and parmesan

Bring a large pan of lightly salted water to a boil. Add the pasta, bring back to a boil, and cook for 8–10 minutes, or until tender but still firm to the bite, then drain thoroughly.

Put the butter and ⅔ cup of the cream in a large, heavy-bottomed pan and bring to a boil. Lower the heat and simmer for 1 minute, or until slightly thickened.

Add the drained pasta to the cream mixture. Place the pan over low heat and toss until the farfalle are thoroughly coated. Season to taste with nutmeg, and salt and pepper, then add the remaining cream and the grated Parmesan. Toss again and serve immediately with extra Parmesan for sprinkling.

VARIATION
For a more substantial dish, melt the butter on its own and add 12 oz/350 g petits pois. Cook for 2–3 minutes, add the cream, and continue as above.

SERVES 4

12 oz/350 g dried radiatori (if
    unavailable, use conchiglie, rotini,
    or fusilli pasta instead)
generous ¾ cup light cream
4 tbsp freshly grated Parmesan cheese,
    plus extra to serve
2 tbsp chopped fresh flatleaf parsley
salt and pepper

PUMPKIN SAUCE

¼ cup unsalted butter
4 oz/115 g white onions or shallots,
    very finely chopped
1 lb 12 oz/800 g pumpkin,
    unprepared weight
pinch of freshly grated nutmeg
salt

RADIATORI AL SUGO DI ZUCCA
radiatori with pumpkin sauce

154

To make the Pumpkin Sauce, melt the butter in a heavy-bottomed pan over low heat. Add the onions, sprinkle with a little salt, cover, and cook, stirring frequently, for 25–30 minutes.

Scoop out and discard the seeds from the pumpkin. Peel and finely chop the flesh. Tip the pumpkin into the pan and season to taste with nutmeg. Cover and cook over low heat, stirring occasionally, for 45 minutes.

Meanwhile, bring a large pan of lightly salted water to a boil. Add the pasta, bring back to a boil, and cook for 8–10 minutes, or until tender but still firm to the bite. Drain thoroughly, reserving about ⅔ cup of the cooking liquid.

Stir the cream, grated Parmesan, and parsley into the Pumpkin Sauce and season to taste with salt and pepper. If the mixture seems a little too thick, add some or all of the reserved cooking liquid. Tip in the pasta and toss for 1 minute. Serve immediately, with extra Parmesan for sprinkling.

VARIATION
Although traditionally made with pumpkin, you could use butternut or acorn squash for this dish.

SERVES 4

12 oz/350 g dried fusilli

3 tbsp olive oil

12 oz/350 g exotic mushrooms, sliced

1 garlic clove, finely chopped

1¾ cups heavy cream

2½ cups crumbled Gorgonzola cheese

salt and pepper

2 tbsp chopped fresh flatleaf parsley,
  to garnish

156 FUSILLI ALLA BOSCAIOLA
fusilli with gorgonzola and mushroom sauce

Bring a large pan of lightly salted water to a boil. Add the pasta, bring back to a boil, and cook for 8–10 minutes, or until tender but still firm to the bite.

Meanwhile, heat the olive oil in a heavy-bottomed pan. Add the mushrooms and cook over low heat, stirring frequently, for 5 minutes. Add the garlic and cook for another 2 minutes.

Add the cream, bring to a boil, and cook for 1 minute, or until slightly thickened. Stir in the cheese and cook over low heat, until it has melted. Do not let the sauce boil once the cheese has been added. Season to taste with salt and pepper and remove the pan from the heat.

Drain the pasta and tip it into the sauce. Toss well to coat, then serve immediately, garnished with the parsley.

COOK'S TIP
Exotic mushrooms have a much earthier flavor than cultivated ones, so they complement the strong taste of the cheese. Porcini are especially delicious, but rather expensive. Portobello or Caesar's mushrooms, if you can find them, would also be a good choice. Otherwise, use cultivated mushrooms, but add 1 oz/25 g dried porcini, which should be soaked for 20 minutes in scant 1 cup hot water, then drained before use.

SERVES 4

3 tbsp olive oil

1 onion, finely chopped

1 garlic clove, finely chopped

generous 1 cup long-grain
  white rice

14 oz/400 g canned chopped tomatoes
  in their juice

pinch of sugar

2½ cups vegetable bouillon

1 tsp dried mint

2 tbsp pine nuts

salt and pepper

lemon wedges, to serve

PILÁFI ME DOMÁTA

tomato pilaf

Heat the oil in a large, heavy-bottomed pan, add the onion and garlic, and cook for 5 minutes, or until softened. Add the rice and cook for 2–3 minutes, stirring all the time, until the rice looks transparent.

Add the tomatoes and their juice, with the sugar, bouillon, mint, and salt and pepper. Bring to a boil, then cover the pan with a tightly fitting lid, and simmer for 15 minutes, or until the rice is tender and the liquid has been absorbed. Do not stir during cooking. When cooked, gently stir in the pine nuts.

Remove the lid, cover the pan with a clean dish towel, replace the lid, and let stand in a warm place for 10 minutes to dry out. Stir with a fork to separate the grains and serve with lemon wedges to squeeze over.

VARIATION
An additional scattering of toasted pine nuts would enhance this pilaf. To prepare these, heat 1 tablespoon of olive oil in a skillet, add ½ cup pine nuts, and cook until golden brown, shaking the pan constantly.

SERVES 6

4 cups vegetable bouillon

3 tbsp unsalted butter

1 red onion, finely chopped

1¾ cups arborio rice

¾ cup dry white wine

generous ½ cup crumbled
  Gorgonzola cheese

generous ½ cup each of freshly grated
  Taleggio, fontina, and Parmesan
  cheese (if Taleggio and/or fontina are
  unavailable, use Swiss cheese instead)

salt and pepper

2 tbsp chopped and sprigs of fresh
  flatleaf parsley, to garnish

RISOTTO AI QUATTRO FORMAGGI
risotto with four cheeses

Pour the bouillon into a large pan and bring to a boil. Lower the heat and simmer gently.

Melt the butter in another large, heavy-bottomed pan. Add the onion and cook over low heat, stirring occasionally, for 5 minutes, or until softened. Add the rice and cook, stirring constantly, for 2–3 minutes, or until all the grains are tho coated and glistening.

Add the wine and cook, stirring constantly, until it has almost completely evaporated. Add a ladleful of the hot bouillon and cook, stirring constantly, until all the bouillon has been absorbed. Continue cooking, stirring and adding the bouillon, a ladleful at a time, for 20 minutes, or until the rice is tender and the liquid has been absorbed.

Remove the pan from the heat and stir in the Gorgonzola, Taleggio, and fontina, and about one fourth of the Parmesan, until melted. Season to taste with salt and pepper. Transfer the risotto to a warmed serving dish, sprinkle with the remaining Parmesan, garnish with the parsley, and serve immediately.

COOK'S TIP
There is a saying in Italy that for a perfect creamy risotto, the rice should just catch on the bottom of the pan. Nevertheless, it is important to use a heavy-bottomed pan, and keep stirring, to prevent the rice from sticking and burning.

SERVES 4

pinch of saffron threads

4 tbsp boiling water

5 cups vegetable bouillon

generous ⅓ cup unsalted butter

2 red onions, finely chopped

2 garlic cloves, finely chopped

1¾ cups arborio rice

⅔ cup dry white wine

scant ½ cup freshly grated
  Parmesan cheese

salt and pepper

RISOTTO ALLA MILANESE
saffron risotto

Place the saffron in a small bowl and add the boiling water. Set aside to soak. Pour the bouillon into a large pan and bring to a boil. Lower the heat and simmer gently.

Melt ¼ cup of the butter in another large, heavy-bottomed pan. Add the onions and garlic and cook over low heat, stirring occasionally, for 5 minutes, or until softened. Add the rice and cook, stirring, until all the grains are coated and glistening.

Add the wine and cook, stirring constantly, until it has almost completely evaporated. Add a ladleful of the hot bouillon and cook, still stirring constantly, until all the bouillon has been absorbed. Continue cooking, stirring and adding the bouillon, a ladleful at a time, for 20 minutes, or until the rice is tender and all the liquid has been absorbed.

Add the saffron liquid, the remaining butter, and the Parmesan, and season to taste with salt and pepper. Cook for 1–2 minutes, or until heated through, then serve immediately.

COOK'S TIP

It is essential to stir the rice constantly for at least the first 10 minutes of cooking in the bouillon and it is safer to do so throughout the whole cooking time. However, as you become a more experienced risotto cook, you will recognize the "feel" of the rice and can stir frequently, rather than constantly, for the last 10 minutes.

SERVES 4

PIZZA DOUGH

3½ cups all-purpose flour, plus extra
   for dusting

2 tsp salt

2 tsp rapid-rise dry yeast

2 tbsp olive oil, plus extra for brushing

¾ cup lukewarm water

FILLING

2 tbsp olive oil

1 red onion, thinly sliced

1 garlic clove, finely chopped

14 oz/400 g canned tomatoes, chopped

2 oz/55 g black olives, pitted
   and chopped

7 oz/200 g mozzarella cheese, drained
   and diced

1 tbsp chopped fresh oregano

salt and pepper

CALZONE

pizza turnover

To make the Pizza Dough, sift the flour and salt into a bowl and stir in the yeast. Make a well in the center and pour in the oil and water. Gradually incorporate the dry ingredients into the liquid, using a wooden spoon or floured hands.

Turn out the dough onto a lightly floured counter and knead well for 5 minutes, or until smooth and elastic. Return to the clean bowl, cover with lightly oiled plastic wrap, and set aside to rise in a warm place for 1 hour, or until doubled in size.

Meanwhile, preheat the oven to 400°F/200°C. To make the filling, heat the olive oil in a skillet. Add the onion and garlic and cook over low heat, stirring occasionally, for 5 minutes, or until softened. Add the tomatoes and cook, stirring occasionally, for another 5 minutes. Stir in the olives and season to taste with salt and pepper. Remove the pan from the heat.

Divide the dough into 4 pieces. Roll out each piece on a lightly floured counter to form an 8-inch/20-cm circle.

Divide the tomato mixture among the circles, spreading it over half of each circle, almost to the edge. Top with the cheese and sprinkle with the oregano. Brush the edge of each circle with a little water and fold over the uncovered sides. Press the edges to seal.

Transfer the turnovers to lightly oiled cookie sheets and bake in the preheated oven for 15 minutes, or until golden and crisp. Remove from the oven and let stand for 2 minutes, then transfer to warmed plates and serve.

SERVES 2

PIZZA DOUGH

2¼ cups all-purpose flour, plus extra
for dusting

1 tsp salt

1 tsp rapid-rise dry yeast

1 tbsp olive oil, plus extra for brushing

6 tbsp lukewarm water

TOPPING

6 tomatoes, thinly sliced

6 oz/175 g mozzarella cheese, drained
and thinly sliced

2 tbsp shredded fresh basil leaves

2 tbsp olive oil

salt and pepper

PIZZA MARGHERITA
cheese and tomato pizza

To make the Pizza Dough, sift the flour and salt into a bowl and stir in the yeast. Make a well in the center and pour in the oil and water. Gradually incorporate the dry ingredients into the liquid, using a wooden spoon or floured hands.

Turn out the dough onto a lightly floured counter and knead well for 5 minutes, or until smooth and elastic. Return to the clean bowl, cover with lightly oiled plastic wrap, and set aside to rise in a warm place for 1 hour, or until doubled in size.

Preheat the oven to 450°F/230°C. Turn out the dough onto a lightly floured counter and punch down. Knead briefly, then cut it in half, and roll out each piece into a circle about ¼ inch/5 mm thick. Transfer to a lightly oiled cookie sheet and push up the edges with your fingers to form a small rim.

For the topping, arrange the tomato and mozzarella slices alternately over the pizza circles. Season to taste with salt and pepper, sprinkle with the basil, and drizzle with the olive oil.

Bake in the preheated oven for 15–20 minutes, or until the crust is crisp and the cheese has melted. Serve immediately.

VARIATION
For Pizza Napoletana, first spread each pizza circle with 4½ teaspoons tomato paste, then top with the tomato and cheese slices. Arrange halved, drained, canned anchovy fillets in a pattern on top, season to taste with pepper, drizzle with olive oil, and bake as above.

VEGETARIAN

SERVES 4–6

1 large eggplant

2 zucchini, thickly sliced

2 onions, cut into small wedges

2 red bell peppers, cored, seeded, and
    coarsely chopped

2 garlic cloves, coarsely chopped

5 tbsp olive oil

1 tbsp chopped fresh thyme

2 eggs, beaten

1¼ cups strained plain yogurt

14 oz/400 g canned chopped tomatoes
    in their juice

generous ½ cup crumbled Greek
    feta cheese

salt and pepper

MOUSSAKÁS LAHANIKÓN
roasted vegetable moussaka

Cut the eggplant into slices about ¼ inch/5 mm thick. Put in a colander, stand it over a large plate, and sprinkle each layer with salt. Cover with a plate and place a heavy weight on top. Let stand for 30 minutes to degorge.

Preheat the oven to 425°F/220°C. Rinse the eggplant slices under cold running water, then pat dry with paper towels. Put the eggplant, zucchini, onions, bell peppers, and garlic in a roasting pan. Drizzle over the oil, toss together, and then sprinkle over the thyme. Season with salt and pepper. Roast in the preheated oven for 30–35 minutes, turning halfway through cooking, until golden brown and tender.

Meanwhile, beat together the eggs, yogurt, and salt and pepper. When the vegetables are cooked, lower the oven temperature to 350°F/180°C.

Put half the vegetables in a layer in a large, ovenproof dish. Spoon over the canned chopped tomatoes and their juice, then add the remaining vegetables. Pour over the yogurt mixture and sprinkle over the feta cheese. Bake in the oven for 45 minutes–1 hour, or until golden brown. Serve hot or cold.

SERVES 6–8

2 tbsp olive oil

2 bunches of scallions, thinly sliced

¼ cup arborio or other short-grain rice

¾ cup vegetable bouillon

1lb 10 oz/750 g zucchini, coarsely
  grated and left to drain in a colander
  for 5–10 mins

4 tbsp chopped fresh flatleaf parsley

2 tbsp chopped fresh mint

3 eggs, beaten

10½ oz/300 g Greek feta cheese

scant ½ cup butter

7 oz/200 g Greek phyllo pie dough

salt and pepper

KOLOKITHÓPITA
zucchini pie

Preheat the oven to 375°F/190°C. Heat the oil in a pan, add the scallions, and cook for 5 minutes, or until softened. Add the rice and cook for 1 minute, stirring to coat in the oil.

Add the bouillon to the pan, bring to boil, and simmer for 15 minutes, or until the bouillon has been absorbed and the rice is tender but still firm to the bite. Remove the pan from the heat and stir in the zucchini. Let cool.

When the mixture has cooled, add the parsley, mint, and eggs. Crumble in the cheese, season with salt and pepper, and mix well together.

Melt the butter and use a little to grease lightly a deep 12 x 8 inch/30 x 20 cm roasting pan.

Cut the phyllo sheets in half widthwise. Take 1 sheet of phyllo and cover the remaining sheets with a damp dish towel. Brush the sheet with a little of the melted butter, and use to line the bottom and sides of the pan. Repeat with half of the phyllo sheets, brushing each with butter.

Spread the zucchini mixture over the phyllo, then top with the remaining phyllo sheets, brushing each with butter and tucking down the edges. Using a sharp knife, score the top layers of the phyllo into 6–8 squares.

Bake the pie in the preheated oven for 35 minutes, or until golden brown. Serve hot.

SERVES 6

2 tbsp olive oil

1 large onion, finely chopped

2 lb 4 oz/1 kg fresh young spinach
leaves, washed, or 1 lb 2 oz/500 g
frozen spinach, thawed

4 tbsp chopped fresh flatleaf parsley

2 tbsp chopped fresh dill

3 eggs, beaten

7 oz/200 g Greek feta cheese

scant ½ cup butter

8 oz/225 g Greek phyllo pie dough

salt and pepper

SPANAKÓPITA
spinach and feta pie

Preheat the oven to 375°F/190°C. To make the filling, heat the oil in a pan, add the onion, and cook for 5–10 minutes, or until softened. Add the fresh spinach if using, with only the water that clings to its leaves after washing, or the frozen spinach, and cook for 2–5 minutes, or until wilted. Remove from the heat and let cool.

When the mixture has cooled, add the parsley, dill, and eggs. Crumble in the cheese, season with salt and pepper, and mix together well.

Melt the butter and use a little to grease lightly a deep 12 x 8 inch/30 x 20 cm roasting pan.

Cut the phyllo sheets in half widthwise. Take 1 sheet of phyllo and cover the remaining sheets with a damp dish towel. Brush it with a little of the melted butter, then use it to line the pan. Repeat with half of the phyllo sheets, brushing each with butter.

Spread the spinach and cheese filling over the phyllo, then top with the remaining phyllo sheets, brushing each with butter and tucking down the edges. Using a sharp knife, score the top layers of the phyllo into 6 squares.

Bake in the preheated oven for 40 minutes, or until golden brown. Serve hot or cold.

Side Dishes
and Salads

MAKES ABOUT 1⅛ CUPS

3–4 large garlic cloves, or to taste

sea salt

2 large egg yolks

1 tsp lemon juice

1¼ cups extra-virgin olive oil

salt and pepper

ALIOLI
garlic mayonnaise

Mash the garlic cloves to a paste with a pinch of sea salt. Put the paste in a food processor, add the egg yolks and lemon juice, and process.

With the motor still running, slowly dribble in the olive oil through the feed tube until an emulsion forms and the sauce thickens. Taste and adjust the seasoning. Transfer to a bowl, cover with plastic wrap, and chill for up to 3 days.

VARIATION
To make Garlic Saffron Sauce, soak a large pinch of saffron in 2 tablespoons of hot water for at least 10 minutes. Follow the recipe above, and add the saffron water after the sauce thickens.

SERVES 4

1 lb/450 g baby zucchini

3 tbsp all-purpose flour

olive oil, for shallow-frying

grated zest and juice of ½ lemon

salt and pepper

sprigs of thyme, to garnish

GREEK GARLIC SAUCE

2 oz/55 g whole blanched almonds

4 tsp fresh white bread crumbs

1 large garlic clove, crushed

1 tsp lemon juice

5 tbsp extra-virgin olive oil

2 tbsp hot water

KOLOKÍTHIA ME SKORDALIÁ
zucchini slices with greek garlic sauce

To make the Greek Garlic Sauce, put the almonds in a food processor and blend until finely ground. Add the bread crumbs, garlic, lemon juice, and salt and pepper, and mix together well. With the machine running, very slowly pour in the oil to form a smooth, thick mixture. When all the oil has been added, blend in the water. Turn the mixture into a serving bowl, cover with plastic wrap, and chill in the refrigerator for at least 2 hours before serving.

Cut the zucchini lengthwise into ¼-inch/5-mm thick strips. Dust with the flour to coat.

Pour enough oil into a large skillet to cover the bottom, heat, then add the zucchini. Cook for 5–10 minutes, or until golden brown, stirring occasionally.

When cooked, add the lemon zest and juice, and season with salt and pepper. Serve the zucchini hot, with the Greek Garlic Sauce spooned on top and garnished with thyme.

SERVES 4–6

large pinch of saffron threads

5 cups hot vegetable bouillon

2 tbsp extra-virgin olive oil

1 large onion, finely chopped

1 large garlic clove, crushed

2 cups short-grain Spanish rice

3½ oz/100 g thin green beans, chopped

⅔ cup frozen peas

salt and pepper

flatleaf parsley, to garnish

ARROZ AZAFRANADO CON VERDURAS
saffron rice with green vegetables

Put the saffron threads in a heatproof bowl and add the hot vegetable bouillon. Set aside to infuse.

Meanwhile, heat the oil in a shallow, heavy-bottomed flameproof casserole over medium-high heat. Add the onion and cook for about 3 minutes, then add the garlic and cook for another 2 minutes, or until the onion is soft but not brown.

Rinse the rice until the water runs clear. Drain, add to the pan, then add the beans. Stir until they are coated with oil. Pour in the bouillon, season with salt and pepper to taste, and bring to a boil. Lower the heat and simmer for 12 minutes, uncovered, and without stirring.

Gently stir in the peas and continue simmering for 8 minutes, or until the liquid has been absorbed and the beans and peas are tender. Taste and adjust the seasoning. Garnish with the parsley and serve.

SERVES 4

5 tbsp olive oil

2 large onions, thinly sliced

1 garlic clove, finely chopped

3 red bell peppers, cored, seeded and cut into strips

3 yellow bell peppers, cored, seeded and cut into strips

12 tomatoes, skinned and chopped

1 tbsp white wine vinegar

salt

PEPERONATA
stewed bell peppers, tomatoes, and onions

Heat the olive oil in a heavy-bottomed skillet. Add the onions, garlic, and bell peppers and cook over low heat, stirring occasionally, for 15 minutes.

Add the tomatoes and season to taste with salt. Stir in the vinegar, cover, and simmer for 30 minutes, or until very tender. Serve immediately.

VARIATION
For Peperonata alla Romana, stir in 1 tablespoon of rinsed and drained capers just before serving.

SERVES 4–6

1 lb/450 g okra

⅔ cup white wine vinegar

3 tbsp olive oil

1 large onion, coarsely chopped

1 large garlic clove, finely chopped

14 oz/400 g canned chopped
  tomatoes in their juice

pinch of sugar

salt and pepper

BÁMIES KOKKINÍSTES
braised okra
with tomatoes

Trim the ends of the okra, but do not cut into the flesh. Put in a bowl, pour over the vinegar, and let stand in a warm place for 30 minutes. Rinse the okra well under cold running water and drain.

Heat the oil in a large skillet, add the onion and garlic, and cook for 5–10 minutes, or until softened. Add the okra and cook for about 5 minutes, stirring occasionally, until it is just beginning to brown.

Add the tomatoes and their juice, with the sugar, and salt and pepper, then simmer for 15–20 minutes, or until the okra is tender and the sauce reduced slightly. Do not boil, or the okra will burst. Serve hot or cold.

MAKES ABOUT SCANT 3 CUPS

4 tbsp olive oil

10 large garlic cloves

5 oz/140 g shallots, chopped

4 large, red bell peppers, cored, seeded, and chopped

2 lb 4 oz/1 kg ripe, fresh tomatoes, chopped, or 2lb 12 oz/1.25 kg good-quality canned chopped tomatoes, in their juice

2 thin strips of freshly pared orange zest

pinch of hot red pepper flakes (optional), to taste

salt and pepper

SALSA DE TOMATES Y PIMIENTOS
tomato and bell pepper sauce

Heat the olive oil in a large, flameproof casserole over medium heat. Add the garlic, shallots, and bell peppers, and cook for about 10 minutes, stirring occasionally, until the bell peppers are soft but not brown.

Add the tomatoes, including the juices if using canned ones, and the orange zest, hot pepper flakes (if using), and salt and pepper to taste. Bring to a boil, then reduce the heat to as low as possible and simmer, uncovered, for 45 minutes, or until the liquid evaporates and the sauce thickens.

Purée the sauce through a food mill. Alternatively, purée in a food processor, then use a wooden spoon to press through a fine strainer. Taste and adjust the seasoning, if necessary. Use immediately, or transfer to a bowl, cover with plastic wrap, and chill for up to 3 days.

SERVES 4

6 oz/175 g dried white beans, such as
  Great Northern, cannellini, black-eye
  peas, or lima beans, covered with
  water and soaked overnight
scant ½ cup olive oil
1 large onion, coarsely chopped
1 large garlic clove, finely chopped
2 carrots, finely chopped
2 celery stalks, thinly sliced

14 oz/400 g canned chopped tomatoes
  in their juice
pinch of sugar
1 tsp dried oregano
1 tbsp chopped fresh flatleaf parsley
salt and pepper

TO SERVE
Greek olives
lemon wedges

FASÓLIA YAHNÍ
greek country beans

Drain the beans, put in a pan, and cover with cold water. Bring to a boil, then boil for 10 minutes. Drain and return to the pan.

Heat the oil in a pan, add the onion and garlic, and cook for 5 minutes, or until softened. Add the carrots and celery and cook for another 10 minutes, or until browned.

Add the beans, tomatoes, sugar, oregano, and parsley, and enough boiling water just to cover the beans. (Do not add salt at this stage, because it toughens the beans.) Bring to a boil, then simmer for 1–1½ hours, or until the beans are really tender and the sauce is thick. The beans should be coated in sauce, but add a little extra water during cooking if the sauce becomes too thick. (The time will vary, depending on the types of bean and how old they are.) Season with salt and pepper.

Let cool slightly before serving with olives and lemon wedges.

SERVES 4–6

4 tbsp olive oil

2 large onions, thinly sliced

4 large garlic cloves, crushed

10½ oz/300 g eggplant, cut into
 ½-inch/1-cm cubes

10½ oz/300 g yellow or green zucchini,
 cut into ½-inch/1-cm cubes

1 large red bell pepper, cored, seeded,
 and chopped

1 large yellow bell pepper, cored, seeded,
 and chopped

1 large green bell pepper, cored, seeded,
 and chopped

2 sprigs of fresh thyme

1 bay leaf

small sprig of young rosemary

scant ½ cup vegetable bouillon

1 lb/450 g large, juicy tomatoes,
 skinned, seeded, and chopped

salt and pepper

sprig of basil, to garnish

PISTO
mixed vegetable stew

Heat 2 tablespoons of the oil in a large, flameproof casserole over medium heat. Add the onions and cook, stirring occasionally, for 5 minutes, or until they start to soften but not brown. Add the garlic and stir around. Reduce the heat to very low.

Meanwhile, heat a skillet over high heat until you can feel the heat rising. Add 1 tablespoon of the oil and the eggplant cubes to make a single layer. Cook, stirring, until they are slightly brown on all sides. Add to the casserole with the onions.

Add another tablespoon of oil to the skillet. Add the zucchini and cook, stirring, until lightly browned all over. Add the zucchini to the casserole. Cook the bell peppers the same way, then add to the casserole.

Stir the thyme, bay leaf, rosemary, and bouillon, and salt and pepper to taste, into the casserole, and bring to a boil. Reduce the heat to very low again, cover, and simmer, stirring occasionally, for 20 minutes, or until the vegetables are very tender and blended.

Remove the casserole from the heat and stir in the tomatoes. Cover and set aside for 10 minutes for the tomatoes to soften. Remove the bay leaf. The pisto is now ready to serve, but it is even better if it is left to cool completely and then served chilled the next day, garnished with basil.

SERVES 4

¼ cup unsalted butter

5 tbsp white granulated sugar

2 tbsp balsamic vinegar

½ cup white wine vinegar

1 lb 7 oz/650 g pearl onions

salt and pepper

CIPOLLINE IN AGRODOLCE
sweet and sour onions

Melt the butter in a heavy-bottomed skillet over low heat. Add the sugar and heat, stirring constantly, until it has dissolved.

Stir in the balsamic and white wine vinegars, then add the onions and season to taste with salt and pepper.

Increase the heat to medium, cover, and cook for 25 minutes, or until the onions are tender and golden. Serve immediately.

SERVES 6

2 lb 4 oz/1 kg potatoes, unpeeled

olive oil, for pan-frying

sea salt

FRITAS
fried potatoes

Scrub the potatoes, pat them dry, and cut into chunky pieces.

Put ½ inch/1 cm olive oil and 1 potato piece in 1 of 2 large, heavy-bottomed skillets over medium-high heat and heat until the potato begins to sizzle. Add the remaining potatoes, without crowding the pans, and cook for 15 minutes, or until golden brown all over and tender. Work in batches, if necessary, keeping the cooked potatoes warm while you cook the remainder.

Use a slotted spoon to transfer the potatoes to a plate covered with crumpled paper towels. Blot off any excess oil and sprinkle with sea salt. Serve immediately.

VARIATION

To make Fried Garlic Potatoes, thinly slice 6 large garlic cloves. Add to the pan with the potatoes, but cook only until they turn brown. Remove with a slotted spoon: if they burn, the oil will taste burnt. Alternatively, cook the potatoes in garlic-flavored olive oil.

SERVES 4

1 lb 9 oz/700 g young carrots

generous 3 tbsp olive oil

scant 2 cups dry white wine

1 tbsp Greek honey

2 sprigs of fresh thyme, chopped

6 sprigs of fresh parsley, chopped

1 bay leaf

2 garlic cloves, finely chopped

1 tbsp coriander seeds, lightly crushed

salt and pepper

fresh herbs, chopped, to garnish

KARÓTA Á LA GRECQUE
greek-style carrots

Cut the carrots in half and then into fourths to form sticks of equal thickness. Put the carrots and all the remaining ingredients in a large pan and bring to a boil, then simmer, uncovered, for 20 minutes, or until the carrots are tender.

Using a slotted spoon, transfer the carrots to a serving dish. Return the cooking liquid to a boil and boil until reduced by about half.

Strain the cooking liquid over the carrots and let cool. When cool, cover with plastic wrap and chill in the refrigerator for 3–4 hours or overnight. Serve at room temperature, garnished with chopped fresh herbs.

SERVES 4

6 tbsp extra-virgin olive oil

2 tbsp fresh lemon juice

1 garlic clove, crushed

pinch of sugar

7 oz/200 g Greek feta cheese

½ head of iceberg lettuce or 1 lettuce
such as romaine or escarole, shredded
or sliced

4 tomatoes, cut into fourths

½ cucumber, sliced

12 Greek black olives, pitted

2 tbsp chopped fresh herbs, such as
oregano, flatleaf parsley, mint,
or basil

salt and pepper

SALÁTA HORIÁTIKI

traditional greek salad

Make the dressing by whisking together the oil, lemon juice, garlic, and sugar, and salt and pepper, in a small bowl. Set aside.

Cut the feta cheese into cubes about 1 inch/2.5 cm square. Put the lettuce, tomatoes, and cucumber in a salad bowl. Scatter over the cheese and toss together.

Just before serving, whisk the dressing, pour over the salad greens, and toss together. Scatter over the olives and chopped herbs and serve.

SERVES 4

10 oz/280 g buffalo mozzarella, drained
  and thinly sliced

8 plum tomatoes, sliced

20 fresh basil leaves

½ cup extra-virgin olive oil

salt and pepper

INSALATA TRICOLORE
three-color salad

Arrange the mozzarella and tomato slices on 4 individual serving plates and season to taste with salt. Set aside in a cool place for 30 minutes.

Sprinkle the basil leaves over the salad and drizzle with the olive oil. Season with pepper and serve immediately.

VARIATIONS

There are dozens of variations to this salad. Before you sprinkle the basil, try adding 24 pitted black olives and 5 drained and chopped anchovies. Alternatively, peel, halve, and pit 2 avocados. Cut the flesh crosswise into thin slices and then arrange these over the mozzarella and tomatoes. Or thinly slice a small white onion and a small red onion, push them out into rings, and arrange them over the salad.

SERVES 6–8

2 tuna steaks, about ¾ inch/2 cm thick

olive oil, for brushing

9 oz/250 g green beans, trimmed

½ cup vinaigrette or garlic vinaigrette
  dressing

2 hearts of lettuce, leaves separated

3 large hard-cooked eggs, cut into fourths

2 juicy vine-ripened tomatoes, cut
  into wedges

1¾ oz/50 g anchovy fillets in oil, drained

2 oz/55 g Niçoise olives, pitted

salt and pepper

fresh basil leaves, torn, to garnish

French bread or other crusty bread,
  to serve

SALADE NIÇOISE
salad niçoise

Heat a ridged cast-iron grill pan over high heat, until you can feel the heat rising from the surface. Brush the tuna steaks with oil, place on the hot pan, oiled-sides down, and cook for 2 minutes. Lightly brush the top sides of the tuna steaks with more oil. Use a pair of tongs to turn the tuna steaks over, then season to taste with salt and pepper. Continue cooking for another 2 minutes for rare or up to 4 minutes for well done. Let cool.

Meanwhile, bring a pan of salted water to a boil. Add the beans to the pan and return to a boil, then boil for 3 minutes, or until tender-crisp. Drain the beans and immediately transfer them to a large bowl. Pour over the vinaigrette and stir together, then let the beans cool in the dressing.

To serve, line a platter with lettuce leaves. Lift the beans out of the bowl, leaving the excess dressing behind, and pile them in the center of the platter. Break the tuna into large flakes and arrange it over the beans. Arrange the hard-cooked eggs and the tomatoes around the side. Arrange the anchovy fillets over the salad, then scatter with the olives and basil. Drizzle the remaining dressing in the bowl over everything and serve with plenty of French bread for mopping up the dressing.

SERVES 4–6

6 large red, orange, or yellow bell peppers, each cut in half lengthwise, broiled, and skinned

4 hard-cooked eggs, shelled

12 anchovy fillets in oil, drained

12 large black olives, pitted

extra-virgin olive oil or garlic-flavored olive oil, for drizzling

sherry vinegar, to taste

salt and pepper

country-style crusty bread, to serve

ENSALADA DE PIMIENTOS
broiled bell pepper salad

Remove any cores and seeds from the broiled bell peppers and cut the flesh into thin strips. Arrange on a serving platter.

Cut the eggs into wedges and arrange over the bell pepper strips, along with the anchovy fillets and olives.

Drizzle oil over the top, then splash with sherry vinegar, adding both to taste. Sprinkle a little salt and pepper over the top and serve with crusty bread.

SERVES 4

3 tbsp extra-virgin olive oil

juice of ½ lemon

2 tsp chopped fresh oregano

pinch of sugar

12 plum tomatoes, sliced

1 very small red onion, very thinly sliced

½ oz/15 g arugula leaves

20 Greek black olives, pitted

7 oz/200 g Greek feta cheese

1 egg

3 tbsp all-purpose flour

2 tbsp olive oil

pepper

DOMATASALÁTA ME FÉTA
tomato salad with feta cheese

Make the dressing by whisking together the extra-virgin olive oil, the lemon juice, oregano, sugar, and black pepper in a pitcher or small bowl. Set aside.

Prepare the salad by arranging the tomatoes, onion, arugula, and olives on 4 individual plates.

Cut the feta cheese into cubes about 1 inch/2.5 cm square. Beat the egg in a dish and put the flour on a separate plate. Toss the cheese in the egg, shake off the excess, and then toss in the flour.

Heat the olive oil in a large skillet, add the cheese, and cook over medium heat, turning over the cubes of cheese until they are golden on all sides.

Scatter the fried feta over the salad. Whisk together the prepared dressing, spoon over the salad, and serve warm.

SERVES 4

5 oz/140 g sun-dried tomatoes in olive oil (drained weight), reserving the oil from the jar

¼ cup coarsely shredded fresh basil

¼ cup coarsely chopped fresh flatleaf parsley

1 tbsp capers, rinsed

1 tbsp balsamic vinegar

1 garlic clove, coarsely chopped

extra olive oil, if necessary

3½ oz/100 g mixed salad greens, such as oak leaf lettuce, baby spinach, and arugula

1 lb 2 oz/500 g smoked mozzarella cheese, sliced

pepper

MOZZARELLA ALLA ROMANA

mozzarella salad with sun-dried tomatoes

Put the sun-dried tomatoes, basil, parsley, capers, vinegar, and garlic in a food processor or blender. Measure the oil from the sun-dried tomatoes jar and make it up to ⅝ cup with more olive oil if necessary. Add it to the food processor or blender and process until smooth. Season to taste with pepper.

Divide the salad greens among 4 individual serving plates. Top with the slices of mozzarella and spoon the dressing over them. Serve immediately.

VARIATION

You can substitute Taleggio cheese or a goat cheese for the mozzarella.

SERVES 4–6

2 red bell peppers

2 green bell peppers

2 yellow or orange bell peppers

½ cup vinaigrette or herb vinaigrette

6 scallions, finely chopped

1 tbsp capers in brine, rinsed

7 oz/200 g soft goat cheese, any
  rind removed

fresh flatleaf parsley, chopped, to serve

broiled bell pepper and goat cheese salad

Preheat the broiler to high. Arrange the bell peppers on a broiler pan, position about 4 inches/ 10 cm from the heat, and broil for 8–10 minutes, turning them frequently, until the skins are charred all over. Transfer the bell peppers to a bowl, cover with a damp dish towel, and let stand until cool enough to handle.

Using a small knife, skin each of the bell peppers. Working over a bowl to catch the juices from inside the bell peppers, cut each one in half and remove the cores and seeds, then cut the flesh into thin strips.

Arrange the bell peppers on a serving platter and spoon over the reserved juices, then add the vinaigrette. Sprinkle over the scallions and capers, then crumble over the cheese. If not serving immediately, cover with plastic wrap and chill until required. Sprinkle with the parsley, to serve.

SERVES 4

6 tbsp extra-virgin olive oil

grated zest of 1 lemon and 2 tbsp
  lemon juice

1 small garlic clove, crushed

pinch of sugar

3 lb/1.3 kg fresh young fava beans, or
  1½ lb/675 g frozen baby fava beans

1½ cups crumbled Greek feta cheese

1 bunch of scallions, thinly sliced

2 tbsp chopped fresh dill or mint

2 hard-cooked eggs, cut into fourths

pepper

TO SERVE

lemon wedges

strained plain yogurt (optional)

SALÁTA ME KOUKIÁ
fava bean salad

Make the dressing by whisking together the oil, lemon zest and juice, garlic, sugar, and black pepper in a small bowl. Set aside.

Shell the fresh fava beans, if using, and cook in boiling salted water for 5–10 minutes, or until tender. If using frozen fava beans, cook in boiling salted water for 4–5 minutes. Drain the cooked beans and put in a salad bowl.

Whisk the dressing and pour over the beans while they are still warm. Spinkle over the feta cheese, add the scallions, and toss together. Sprinkle over the chopped dill and arrange the egg wedges around the edge.

Serve warm with lemon wedges, and a bowl of yogurt to spoon on top, if desired.

COOK'S TIP

If using mint in this salad, sprinkle a pinch of sugar over it as you chop to bring out its full aroma.

Desserts

SERVES 4

¾ cup superfine sugar

thinly pared zest of 1 lemon

2-inch/5-cm piece of cinnamon stick

scant 1 cup water

scant 1 cup Marsala

2 lb/900 g Morello cherries, pitted

⅔ cup heavy cream

CILIEGE AL MARSALA
marsala cherries

Put the sugar, lemon zest, cinnamon stick, water, and Marsala in a heavy-bottomed pan and bring to a boil, stirring constantly. Lower the heat and simmer for 5 minutes. Remove the cinnamon stick.

Add the Morello cherries, cover, and simmer gently for 10 minutes. Using a slotted spoon, transfer the cherries to a bowl.

Return the pan to the heat and bring to a boil over high heat. Boil for 3–4 minutes, or until thick and syrupy. Pour the syrup over the cherries and set aside to cool, then chill for at least 1 hour.

Whisk the cream until stiff peaks form. Divide the cherries and syrup among 4 individual dishes or glasses, top with the cream, and serve.

SERVES 4–6

4 large, juicy oranges

1¼ cups superfine sugar

1¼ cups water

4–6 tbsp slivered almonds, toasted,
  to serve

NARANJAS DE VALENCIA
CON CARAMELO
valencia caramel oranges

Working over a heatproof bowl to catch any juices, and using a small serrated knife, pare the oranges, taking care not to leave any of the bitter-tasting pith. Use the knife to remove the orange segments, cutting between the membranes. Squeeze the empty membranes over the bowl to extract as much juice as possible. Discard the membranes and set the segments and juice aside.

Put the sugar and ⅔ cup of the water into a small, heavy-bottomed pan over medium-high heat. Stir until the sugar dissolves, then bring to a boil and boil, without stirring, until the syrup turns a rich golden brown.

Pour the remaining water into the pan (stand back because the caramel will splatter). Stir again until the caramel dissolves. Remove from the heat and let the caramel cool slightly, then pour over the oranges. Stir to blend the orange juice into the caramel. Let the oranges cool completely, then cover with plastic wrap and chill for at least 2 hours before serving.

Just before serving, sprinkle the caramel oranges with the toasted slivered almonds.

SERVES 6

¼ cup unsalted butter, plus extra
  for greasing

6 large peaches

scant ⅔ cup ground almonds

1 cup coarsely crushed amaretti

1 tbsp Amaretto liqueur

½ tsp grated lemon zest

1 tsp unsweetened cocoa

2 tsp confectioners' sugar

scant 1 cup medium-dry
  white wine

PESCHE RIPIENE ALLA PIEMONTESE
stuffed piemont peaches

Preheat the oven to 350°F/180°C. Grease an ovenproof dish with butter. Cut the peaches in half, then remove and discard the pits. Widen the central cavity by cutting away and reserving some of the flesh in a bowl.

Add the almonds, amaretti, Amaretto, lemon zest, and half the butter to the reserved peach flesh and mash with a fork. Fill the peach cavities with this mixture and place them in the dish.

Dot the peaches with the remaining butter and sprinkle with the unsweetened cocoa and confectioners' sugar. Pour the wine into the dish and bake in the preheated oven for 30 minutes, or until golden. Serve immediately.

COOK'S TIP
Use white peaches if you can find them, because they have the sweetest and most succulent flavor. However, whether using white or yellow, do make sure the peaches are really ripe.

SERVES 4

⅔ cup fresh orange juice

6 tbsp Greek honey

12 ready-to-eat dried figs

1½ oz/40 g shelled pistachios,
  finely chopped

1 oz/25 g ready-to-eat dried apricots,
  very finely chopped

1 tsp sesame seeds

strained plain yogurt, to serve

SÍKA FOURNÓU ME MÉLI
baked stuffed honey figs

Preheat the oven to 325°F/160°C. Put the orange juice and 5 tablespoons of the honey in a pan and heat gently until the honey has dissolved. Add the figs and simmer for 10 minutes, or until softened. Remove from the heat and let cool in the liquid.

Meanwhile, prepare the filling. Put the nuts, apricots, sesame seeds, and remaining tablespoon of honey in a bowl, and mix together well.

Using a slotted spoon, remove the figs from the cooking liquid and reserve the liquid. Cut a slit at the top of each fig, where the stem joins. Using your fingers, plump up the figs and stuff each fig with about 1 teaspoon of the filling mixture. Close the top of each fig and place in an ovenproof dish. Pour over the reserved cooking liquid.

Bake the figs in the preheated oven for 10 minutes, or until hot. Serve warm or cold, with the sauce and strained yogurt.

MAKES 16–20

1 cup all-purpose flour,
  plus extra for dusting
3 tbsp unsalted butter, melted
1 tbsp Spanish cream sherry
½ tsp vanilla extract
pinch of salt
1 small egg, very lightly beaten
olive oil, for deep-frying

TO DECORATE

2 tbsp confectioners' sugar
½ tsp ground cinnamon
pinch of ground ginger

PASTELES FRITOS
deep-fried sweet pastries

Put the flour in a bowl and make a well in the center. Add the butter, cream sherry, vanilla extract, salt, and 1 tablespoon of the beaten egg, and mix together until a dough forms. Knead the dough in the bowl until it is smooth. Shape into a ball and wrap in plastic wrap. Set aside at room temperature for 15 minutes.

On a lightly floured counter, roll out half the dough very thinly. Use a 2¼-inch/5.5-cm fluted cookie cutter and cut out 8–10 circles, re-rolling the trimmings. Repeat the process with the remaining dough.

Heat 2 inches/5 cm of oil in a heavy-bottomed skillet over high heat to 350°F/180°C, or until a cube of day-old bread turns brown in 30 seconds. Add 5–6 dough circles, without overcrowding the pan, and cook for 45 seconds, then turn them over with a large slotted spoon, and continue cooking, until the circles are puffed on both sides and golden brown. Transfer to crumpled paper towels and drain very well. Take care: they are delicate and can break easily. Repeat with the remaining dough circles.

While the pastries are still hot, mix the confectioners' sugar, cinnamon, and ginger together. Use a fine strainer to sift the mixture over the warm pastries. They will keep in an airtight container for up to 3 days.

MAKES 12

scant ½ cup unsalted butter, plus extra
   for greasing
2⅓ cups finely chopped walnut pieces
generous ¼ cup superfine sugar
1 tsp ground cinnamon

½ tsp ground cloves
8 oz/225 g Greek phyllo pie dough
⅔ cup Greek honey
2 tsp lemon juice
⅔ cup water

BAKLAVÁS
sweet walnut pastries

Preheat the oven to 425°F/220°C. Melt the butter and use a little to grease lightly a deep
10 x 7 inch/25 x 18 cm roasting pan.

To make the filling, put the walnuts, sugar, cinnamon, and cloves in a bowl and mix
together well.

Cut the phyllo sheets in half widthwise. Take 1 sheet of phyllo and use to line the pan. Cover
the remaining sheets with a damp dish towel. Brush the sheet with a little of the melted butter.
Repeat with half of the phyllo sheets, then sprinkle over the walnut filling. Top with the
remaining phyllo sheets, brushing each with butter, and tucking down the edges. Using a
sharp knife, cut the top layers of the phyllo into 12 diamond shapes or square shapes.

Bake in the preheated oven for 10 minutes, then lower the oven temperature to 350°F/180°C
and bake for another 20 minutes, or until golden brown.

Just before the pastries have cooked, make the honey syrup. Put the honey, lemon juice, and
the water in a pan and simmer for 5 minutes, or until combined. Set aside.

When the pastries are cooked, remove from the oven and pour over the honey syrup. Let cool.
Before serving, cut along the marked lines again to divide into pieces.

SERVES 12–14

4 oz/115 g hazelnuts

4 oz/115 g almonds

⅔ cup chopped candied peel

¼ cup ready-to-eat dried apricots,
   finely chopped

2 oz/55 g candied pineapple,
   finely chopped

grated zest of 1 orange

generous ½ cup all-purpose flour

2 tbsp unsweetened cocoa

1 tsp ground cinnamon

¼ tsp ground coriander seeds

¼ tsp freshly grated nutmeg

¼ tsp ground cloves

generous ½ cup superfine sugar

generous ½ cup clear honey

confectioners' sugar, to decorate

PANFORTE DI SIENA
tuscan cake

Preheat the oven to 350°F/180°C. Line a cake pan with baking parchment. Spread out the hazelnuts on a cookie sheet and toast in the preheated oven for 10 minutes, or until golden brown. Tip them onto a dish towel and rub off the skins. Meanwhile, spread out the almonds on a cookie sheet and toast in the oven for 10 minutes, or until golden. Watch carefully after 7 minutes, because they can burn easily. Lower the oven temperature to 300°F/150°C. Remove from the oven, chop all the nuts, and place in a large bowl.

Add the candied peel, apricots, pineapple, and orange zest to the nuts, and mix well. Sift together the flour, cocoa, cinnamon, coriander, nutmeg, and cloves into the bowl and mix well.

Put the sugar and honey into a pan and set over low heat, stirring, until the sugar has dissolved. Bring to a boil and cook for 5 minutes, or until thickened and beginning to darken. Stir the nut mixture into the pan and remove from the heat.

Spoon the mixture into the prepared cake pan and smooth the surface with the back of a damp spoon. Bake in the oven for 1 hour, then transfer to a wire rack to cool in the pan.

Carefully remove the cake from the pan and peel off the baking parchment. Just before serving, dredge the top with confectioners' sugar. Cut into thin wedges to serve.

COOK'S TIP
You can make this cake up to 2 weeks in advance. Store in an airtight container.

SERVES 8–12

PIE DOUGH

generous 2¼ cups all-purpose flour,
   plus extra for dusting

pinch of salt

1½ tsp superfine sugar

⅔ cup unsalted butter, cut into cubes

3–4 tbsp cold water

FILLING

1⅔ cups cottage cheese, cream cheese,
   or ricotta

6 tbsp Greek honey

3 eggs, beaten

½ tsp ground cinnamon

grated zest and juice of 1 lemon

slices of fresh lemon, to decorate

230 SIPHNÓPITTA
honey and lemon tart

To make the pie dough, put the flour, salt, sugar, and butter in a food processor. Mix in short bursts, until the mixture resembles fine bread crumbs. Sprinkle over the water and mix together, until the mixture forms a smooth dough. Alternatively, make the dough in a bowl and rub in with your hands. The dough can be used straight away but is better if you let it rest in the refrigerator, wrapped in waxed paper or foil, for about 30 minutes before use.

Preheat the oven to 400°F/200°C. If using cottage cheese to make the filling, push the cheese through a strainer into a bowl. Add the honey to the cheese and beat until smooth. Add the eggs, cinnamon, and lemon zest and juice and mix together well.

On a lightly floured counter, roll out the dough and use to line a 9-inch/23-cm tart pan. Place on a cookie sheet and line with waxed paper. Weigh down with pie weights and bake in the preheated oven for 15 minutes. Remove the weights and waxed paper and bake for another 5 minutes, or until the bottom is firm but not brown.

Lower the oven temperature to 350°F/180°C. Pour the filling into the tart shell and bake in the oven for 30 minutes, or until set. Remove from the oven and let cool. Decorate with lemon slices and serve cold.

SERVES 6–8

PIE DOUGH

1¾ cups all-purpose flour, plus extra
   for dusting

3 tbsp superfine sugar

½ cup unsalted butter, chilled and diced

1 egg yolk

salt

FILLING

2 cups ricotta cheese

½ cup heavy cream

2 eggs, plus 1 egg yolk

scant ½ cup superfine sugar

finely grated zest of 1 lemon

finely grated zest of 1 orange

CROSTATA DI RICOTTA

ricotta cheesecake

To make the pie dough, sift the flour with the sugar and a pinch of salt onto a counter and make a well in the center. Add the diced butter and the egg yolk to the well and, using your fingertips, gradually work in the flour mixture, until fully incorporated. Gather up the dough and knead very lightly. Cut off about one-fourth, wrap in plastic wrap, and chill in the refrigerator. Press the remaining dough into the bottom of a loose-bottomed nonstick tart pan. Cover with plastic wrap and chill for 30 minutes.

Preheat the oven to 375°F/190°C. To make the filling, beat the ricotta with the cream, eggs and extra egg yolk, sugar, lemon zest, and orange zest. Cover with plastic wrap and set aside in the refrigerator until required.

Prick the bottom of the tart shell all over with a fork. Line with foil, fill with pie weights, and bake blind in the preheated oven for 15 minutes. Remove the tart shell from the oven, leaving the oven on, and take out the weights and foil. Stand the pan on a wire rack and set aside to cool.

Spoon the ricotta mixture into the tart shell and smooth the surface. Roll out the reserved pie dough on a lightly floured counter and cut it into strips. Arrange the strips over the filling in a lattice pattern, brushing the overlapping ends with water so that they stick.

Bake in the oven for 30–35 minutes, or until the top of the cheesecake is golden and the filling has set. Remove from the oven and cool on a wire rack before lifting off the side of the pan. Cut into wedges to serve.

SERVES 4–6

1 cup mascarpone cheese

2 tbsp finely ground coffee beans

2 tbsp confectioners' sugar

3 oz/85 g semisweet chocolate, finely grated

1½ cups heavy cream, plus extra to decorate

Marsala wine, to serve

234 SEMIFREDDO AL CIOCCOLATO
chilled chocolate dessert

Beat the mascarpone with the coffee and confectioners' sugar, until thoroughly combined.

Set aside 4 teaspoons of the grated chocolate and stir the remainder into the cheese mixture with 5 tablespoons of the cream.

Whisk the remaining cream until it forms soft peaks. Stir 1 tablespoon of the mascarpone mixture into the cream to slacken it, then fold the cream into the remaining mascarpone mixture with a figure-eight action.

Spoon the mixture into a freezerproof container and place in the freezer for about 3 hours.

To serve, scoop the chocolate dessert into sundae glasses and drizzle with a little Marsala. Top with whipped cream and decorate with the reserved grated chocolate. Serve immediately.

COOK'S TIP
Do not freeze the mixture for longer than 3 hours, or it will lose its texture.

SERVES 6

generous 2 cups milk

½ orange, with 2 long, thin pieces
    of zest removed and reserved

1 vanilla bean, split, or ½ tsp
    vanilla extract

scant 1 cup superfine sugar

4 tbsp water

unsalted butter, for greasing

3 large eggs, plus 2 large egg yolks

FLAN DE LECHE ACARMELADO
spanish caramel custard

Pour the milk into a pan with the orange zest and vanilla. Bring to a boil, then remove from the heat and stir in ½ cup of the sugar. Set aside for at least 30 minutes to infuse.

Preheat the oven to 325°F/160°C. Put the remaining sugar and 4 tablespoons of water in a pan over medium-high heat. Stir until the sugar dissolves, then boil without stirring, until the caramel turns deep golden-brown.

Immediately remove the pan from the heat and squeeze in a few drops of orange juice to stop the cooking. Pour into a lightly buttered 5-cup soufflé dish and swirl to cover the bottom. Set aside.

When the milk has infused, return the pan to the heat and bring the milk to a simmer. Beat the whole eggs and egg yolks together in a heatproof bowl. Pour the warm milk into the eggs, whisking constantly. Strain this mixture into the soufflé dish. Place the soufflé dish in a roasting pan and pour in enough boiling water to come halfway up the sides of the dish. Bake in the preheated oven for 75–90 minutes, or until set and a knife inserted in the center comes out clean.

Remove the soufflé dish from the roasting pan and set aside to cool completely. Cover with plastic wrap and chill overnight.

To serve, run a metal spatula around the side of the dish, invert onto a serving plate with a rim to catch the juices, then shake firmly to release.

SERVES 6

1 lb/450 g sweet chestnuts

1¼ cups milk

1 bay leaf

2 inch/5 cm cinnamon stick

generous ¾ cup superfine sugar

2 large egg yolks

½ tsp vanilla extract

4 tbsp dark rum

unsalted butter, for greasing

⅔ cup heavy cream, plus extra
  to decorate

SPUMA DI CASTAGNE
chestnut mousse

Use a knife to cut a slit in the rounded side of the shell of each chestnut, then place in a pan. Add water to cover and bring to a boil. Boil for 5 minutes, then remove with a slotted spoon. When cool enough to handle, but still warm, remove the shells. The inner skins should peel off easily at the same time.

Place the shelled chestnuts in a heavy-bottomed pan, then add the milk, bay leaf, cinnamon, and half the sugar. Bring to a boil, stirring to dissolve the sugar. Lower the heat, cover, and simmer gently, stirring occasionally, for 40 minutes, or until the chestnuts are tender. Remove the pan from the heat and set aside to cool.

Preheat the oven to 350°F/180°C. Remove and discard the bay leaf and cinnamon from the pan and transfer the contents to a food processor or blender. Process to a smooth purée. Alternatively, rub the mixture through a strainer with a wooden spoon, or purée in a food mill.

Beat the yolks with the remaining sugar, until fluffy and the whisk leaves a trail when lifted. Stir in the vanilla and rum, then fold in the chestnut purée. Whip the cream in a separate bowl until it forms stiff peaks, then fold into the purée.

Lightly grease 6 ovenproof molds with butter and spoon the chestnut mixture into them. Stand the molds on a cookie sheet and bake in the preheated oven for 10–15 minutes, or until just set. Remove from the oven, and set the molds aside to cool to room temperature before serving. Alternatively, cover with plastic wrap and chill until required. To serve, turn out the molds onto individual plates and pipe a border of heavy cream around the bottom of each one.

SERVES 4–6
3–4 lemons
generous 1 cup water

1 cup superfine sugar
Spanish cava, chilled, to serve

SORBETE DE LIMÓN CON CAVA
lemon sherbet with cava

Roll the lemons on a counter, pressing firmly to release as much juice as possible. Pare off a few strips of zest and reserve for decoration, then finely grate the zest from 3 lemons. Squeeze the juice from as many of the lemons as necessary to give ¾ cup.

Put the water and sugar in a heavy-bottomed pan over medium-high heat and stir to dissolve the sugar. Bring to a boil, without stirring, and boil for 2 minutes. Remove from the heat, stir in the grated lemon zest, cover, and let stand for 30 minutes, or until cool.

When the mixture is cool, stir in the lemon juice. Strain into an ice-cream maker and freeze according to the manufacturer's instructions. (Alternatively, strain the mixture into a freezerproof container and freeze for 2 hours, or until mushy and freezing around the edges. Tip into a bowl and beat. Return to the freezer and repeat the process twice more.) Remove the sherbet from the freezer to soften 10 minutes before serving.

To serve, scoop into 4–6 tall glasses, decorate with the reserved zest, if using, and top off with cava.

VARIATION
Spaniards also serve lemon sherbet in frozen hollow lemon shells. To do this, slice the tops off 4–6 lemons and use a sharp teaspoon to scoop out the flesh. Spoon the almost-frozen sherbet into the lemons and place in the freezer upright until frozen.

SERVES 4–6

3 large blood oranges

generous ⅓ cup lowfat milk

generous ⅓ cup light cream

⅔ cup superfine sugar

4 large egg yolks

scant 2 cups heavy cream

⅛ tsp vanilla extract

almond cookies, to serve

242 HELADO DE NARANJAS DE SANGRE
blood-orange ice cream

Thinly pare the zest from 2 oranges, reserving a few strips for decoration, and finely grate the zest from the third. Squeeze the oranges to give ½ cup juice and set aside.

Pour the milk and cream into a pan with the pared orange zest. Bring to a boil, then remove from the heat. Set aside for at least 30 minutes to infuse.

Select a heatproof bowl that fits over the pan without touching the bottom. Put the sugar and egg yolks in the bowl and beat until thick and creamy. Return the milk mixture to the heat and bring to a simmer, then pour onto the eggs and whisk until blended. Wash the pan and put a small amount of water in the bottom. Place over medium heat and bring the water to a simmer. Lower the heat. Put the bowl on top and stir for 20 minutes, or until a thick custard forms that coats the back of the spoon; the water must not touch the bottom of the bowl, or the eggs might scramble.

Strain the mixture into a clean bowl. Stir in the finely grated orange zest and set aside for 10 minutes. Stir in the reserved juice, and the heavy cream and vanilla extract.

Transfer to an ice-cream maker and freeze following the manufacturer's instructions. (Alternatively, strain the mixture into a freezerproof container and freeze for 2 hours, or until freezing around the edges. Tip into a bowl and beat. Return to the freezer and repeat the process twice more.) Remove from the freezer to soften 15 minutes before serving. Decorate with strips of the reserved zest and serve with almond cookies.

SERVES 4

1¼ cups heavy cream

⅔ cup strained plain yogurt

2 tbsp milk

3 tbsp Greek honey

a few drops of green food coloring
  (optional)

scant ½ cup shelled, unsalted pistachios

PISTACHIO PRALINE

oil, for brushing

¾ cup granulated sugar

3 tbsp water

scant ¾ cup shelled, whole,
  unsalted pistachios

PAGOTÓ FISTÍKIA
pistachio ice cream

Turn on an ice-cream maker or set the freezer to its lowest setting. Put the cream, yogurt, milk, and honey in a bowl and mix together. Add a few drops of green food coloring to tint the mixture pale green, if desired, and stir in well. Pour the mixture into an ice-cream maker and freeze according to the manufacturer's instructions.

Meanwhile, put the pistachios for the ice cream in a food processor and chop very finely. Stir the nuts into the ice cream just before it freezes firmly.

Alternatively, pour the ice-cream mixture into a shallow container and freeze, uncovered, for 1–2 hours, or until beginning to set around the edges. Turn the mixture into a bowl and, with a fork, stir until smooth, then add the nuts. Return to the freezer container, cover, and freeze for another 2–3 hours, or until firm.

To make the Pistachio Praline, brush a cookie sheet with oil. Put the sugar and water in a pan and heat gently, stirring, until the sugar has dissolved, then let it bubble gently, without stirring, for 6–10 minutes, or until lightly golden brown.

Remove the pan from the heat and stir in the nuts. Pour the mixture onto the cookie sheet and spread out evenly. Let cool for 1 hour, or until hardened. When it is hard, crush it in a food processor or in a plastic bag with a hammer.

Remove the ice cream from the freezer to soften 30 minutes before serving. Scatter the praline over the ice cream before serving.

MAKES 4 GLASSES

scant 2 cups water

scant ⅔ cup granulated sugar

scant 1 cup lemon juice

grated zest of 1 lemon

lemon slices, to decorate

GRANITA AL LIMONE
lemon ice

Heat the water in a heavy-bottomed pan over low heat. Add the sugar and stir until it has completely dissolved. Bring to a boil, remove the pan from the heat, and set the syrup aside to cool.

Stir the lemon juice and zest into the syrup. Pour the mixture into a freezerproof container and place in the freezer for 3–4 hours.

To serve, remove the container from the freezer and dip the bottom into hot water. Turn out the ice block and chop coarsely, then place in a food processor and process until it forms small crystals (granita means "granular"). Spoon into glasses, decorate with lemon slices, and serve immediately.

VARIATIONS
Many different fruit syrups can be used to flavor these ices—oranges, mandarins, pink grapefruit, or mangoes. Simply substitute the juice. You can add extra flavor with a splash of liqueur or include herbs, such as lemon balm or elderflower, when making the syrup (strain before pouring into the freezer container). Coffee ice made with espresso coffee instead of fruit juice, with or without a dash of liqueur, is also delicious.

COOK'S TIP
An ordinary blender may not be sufficiently robust to process the ice, which may damage the blades. A good-quality food processor is recommended.

MAKES 12–15 GLASSES

scant ½ cup Spanish brandy

4 large lemons, sliced and cut
    into fourths

4 large oranges, sliced and cut
    into fourths

2 limes, sliced and cut into fourths

2 peaches, pitted and sliced (optional)

two standard-sized (750 ml) bottles of
    full-bodied Spanish red wine, chilled

scant 1 cup superfine sugar, plus extra
    to taste

ice cubes, to serve

248   SANGRÍA
sangria

Put the brandy and half the citrus fruit and peach slices, if using, in a bowl and use a wooden spoon to crush the fruit into the brandy. Cover with plastic wrap and chill for at least 2 hours. Cover the remaining fruit slices and chill until required.

Pour the brandy and fruit into a large serving pitcher, add the wine and the sugar, and stir until the sugar has dissolved. Taste and add extra sugar, if desired, then add the ice cubes. Place a mixture of the reserved fruit slices in glasses and pour over the Sangria, including some of the brandy-soaked fruit.

MAKES 2 CUPS

¾ cup cold water

2 tsp sugar for medium sweetness, or
  according to taste

2 heaping tsp fine-ground coffee

glasses of ice water, to serve

ELLINIKÓS KAFÉS
greek coffee

Put the water, and the sugar according to taste, in a "briki" (a small, tall, metal container with a long handle and a lip for pouring) or a small pan. Bring to a boil and then, before it overflows, remove from the heat, and stir in the coffee.

Return to the heat. As soon as the coffee forms a foam and boils to the top of the briki, remove from the heat, and tap the sides of the briki with a teaspoon, until the coffee subsides a little.

Repeat the boiling of the coffee and tapping of the briki for a second time.

Return to the heat for a third time and just before the coffee boils over, remove from the heat and, using a teaspoon, spoon the foam into 2 coffee cups. Pour the coffee into the cups, being careful not to disturb the foam on top of each cup. Serve with glasses of ice water.

MAKES 1 CUP

2 tbsp Amaretto

1 cup hot black coffee

1 tbsp heavy cream

252 ESPRESSO AMARETTO
amaretto coffee

Pour the Amaretto into the cup of coffee and stir so that the flavor mixes in well with the coffee.

Hold a teaspoon, rounded side upward, against the side of the cup with the tip just touching the surface of the coffee. Pour the cream over the back of the spoon so that it floats on top of the coffee. Serve immediately.

Index